THOUGH YOU SLAY ME

ONE WOMAN'S FAITH
AND DETERMINATION
TO SURVIVE THE
DESTRUCTION AND
DEVASTATION OF WAR
AND GIVE HOPE
TO OTHERS

RITA HARRIS

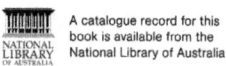
A catalogue record for this book is available from the National Library of Australia

Content Guidance: This book contains war events that readers may find distressing including violence, torture and sexual assault. Please read with care.

THOUGH YOU SLAY ME
Copyright 2024 ©Rita Harris
Published by Star Label Publishing
P.O. Box 1511, Buderim, QLD, Australia
publishing@starlabel.com.au

Editing: Mandy Chandler
Cover, editing and interior design: Rebecca Moore

All rights reserved. No part of this publication may be reproduced in any form; stored in a retrieval system; or transmitted, or used in any other form; or by any other means without prior written permission of the publisher (except for brief quotes for the purpose of review or promotion).

The views expressed here-in remain the sole responsibility of the author, who exempts the publisher from all liability. The author and publisher do not assume responsibility for any loss, damage, or disruption caused by the contents, errors or omissions, whether such contents, errors, or omissions result from opinion, negligence, accident, or any other cause, and hereby disclaim any and all liability to any party.

ISBN: 978-0-6459337-7-2

For my mother, Esther.
Though I never saw her face,
she is forever in my heart.

I saw skulls. I saw dogs eating bodies. I saw bloated bodies. I saw exploding bodies. I saw women dead. I saw children dead. I saw babies dead. I saw a war ... I can't apologise for war. Everybody has had a war.

— John Toussaint Richardson
(Taylor's adviser)

TABLE OF CONTENTS

List of acronyms...14
Preface 16
Prologue..17
Introduction..20

Part 1 1970s–1980 Peace in the village......................23
    The beginning...23
    Rocking my dolls 24
    Grandma 25
    Dreams of being a farmer 27
    The gilded age..29
    School 31
    God's blessings...33
    A new calling 33
    Womanhood 34
    Carefree teenage years..35
    Hide-and-seek 36
    Young love..37
    An unexpected pregnancy......................................37
    Dark clouds gather 40
    Sovereignty and independence..............................42
    Introducing a two-party system 42
    Novel approach to foreign policy 43
    Disillusionment and dissent 44
    The Rice Riots..45

The assassination of Tolbert and the rise of
Samuel Doe 47
Currying favour with the US....................................48

Part 2 1980 Gardnersville 49
Uncle Bennie 49
The house in Gardnersville 50
A warm welcome..50
Homesickness 51
Christopher...53
School in Monrovia 53
A harmonious life 55

Part 3 1980–1985 Trouble brewing....................57
Tense times 57
1985 Election..58
The Quiwonkpa coup..59
Doe's inauguration 61

Part 4 1989–1992 The war begins........................63
Charles Taylor attacks..63
Food as an instrument of war 65
Appeals for international aid....................................66
General Babangida...67
NPFL splits 68
Caught in the crossfire...69
The Monrovian Church Massacre 72
Exodus from Monrovia..73

7

On the road to Bong County 74
Adam and Eve Creek 77
Life in Cuttington 79
On the road again 84
Ma Fanta Fofana saves my life – twice 86
Gbarnga..88
Ornekel...89
Caldwell..90
Diplomacy fails...91
ECOMOG forces enter Liberia 93
The Dukuly Prophecy 95
Assassination of Samuel K. Doe 95
ECOMOG appoints Dogonyaro 97
Operation Liberty..97
The Bakamo ceasefire 98
A fragile peace 99
Plans for disarmament...100
National Patriotic Reconstruction Assembly
Government (NPRAG)..101
The United Liberation Movement for
Democracy 102
Hopes dashed 104

Part 5 1992–1993 No end to war 109
The Black Berets..109
Trouble brewing...110
The Small Boys Unit 112
Operation Octopus..114

    Nuns massacred in Gardnersville 117
    Widespread terror and confusion......................... 118
    ECOWAS meets in Abuja..................................... 118
    The AFL makes an example................................. 119
    ECOMOG bombs fall on civilians......................... 119
    Early 1993.. 120
    Refugees flow into neighbouring countries 121
    The Nimba Redemption Council of Liberia
    (NRCL).. 121
    Aftermath.. 122
    The Cotonou Peace Accord.................................. 123
    The United Nations Observer Mission in
    Liberia... 124

Part 6 1993–1995 Monrovia............................... 127
    Return to Monrovia... 127
    A city in ruins.. 128
    Reunion.. 129
    Naomi... 132
    ECOMOG: Friend or foe?.................................... 133
    Life in Monrovia under ECOMOG..................... 134
    Marco Carto.. 145
    News of my grandparents................................... 149

Part 7 1994–1996 The struggle for peace................ 151
    A humanitarian crisis... 151
    Liberia in a desperate state.................................. 154
    The Abuja Agreement... 155

A turn for the worse...156
The US Marines...159
Sierra Leone...159
Charles Taylor wins election....................................162

Part 8 1996–2012 Love comes calling...................165
Phillip Harris..165
Phillip's story...170
Phil's proposal 172
Phil meets my family..174
Our wedding..174
A prophecy fulfilled..175
Meeting Phillip's family 176
Maureen..178
Life with Phil...178
Learning English from Phyllis 180
Travelling grace...181
Chris 182
Homesickness 183
A global community 185
Life on UN bases 186
A little push 186
Time to settle down 188
Allergic to books 188
Working as a carer 190
Itchy feet 192
Finding my niche..193

Part 9 2013–2023 A fortunate life 195
    The Isle of Wight 195
    Doing what I love 195
    Not one instance of prejudice or racism 196
    A loving community 197
    My husband – a true gentleman 198
    Marriage 198
    Family 199
    Faith 199
    Thoughts of home 201
    God's plan 202
    Hopes and regrets 203
    Keeping my word 204
    Finding joy in the little things 205
    Lessons learned 205

Epilogue – Lament for Liberia 207
    Poverty 207
    Education disaster 209
    Corruption 210
    Drug addiction 211
    Prostitution 214
    Crime 216
    Rape 217
    Illegal emigration 218
    Still bleeding 218
    Liberia's indomitable spirit 219
    Once a Liberian, always a Liberian 220

A Time for Everything..221
Arise and shine..223

Appendix 226
Liberia's diverse population..............................226
The Kpelle..227
The Kru...227
The Grebo...228
The Bassa 230
The Dei..231
The Gio (Dan) 231
The Mano 233
The Krahn 233
The Sapo 234
The Gola 234
The Gbandi 235
The Loma..235
The Kissi 236
The Vai..237
The Kuwaa 238
The Mandé 238
The Americo-Liberians 239

Author Notes 240
Liberian Culture..240
Hospitality...240
Place names 240
Sport..241

First female head of state 241
Liberian women 242
Holidays in Liberia 242
Transport 244
Careers 244
Social life..245

Author Bio..246
Bibliography..247
Timeline of events.......................................249

LIST OF ACRONYMS

ACS	American Colonisation Society
AFL	Armed Forces of Liberia
BP	Years before present
CRS	Catholic Relief Society
ECOMOG	ECOWAS Ceasefire Monitoring Group
ECOWAS	Economic Community of West African States
FIFA	Fédération Internationale de football association (French for 'International Association Football Federation')
GHI	Global Hunger Index
IDP	Internally displaced people
IGNU	Interim Government of National Unity
INPFL	Independent National Patriotic Front of Liberia
JFK	John F. Kennedy
LAMCO	Liberian American Swedish Mining Company
LAP	Liberian Action Party
LDF	Lofa Defence Force
LPC	Liberian Peace Council
LPMC	Liberia Produce Marketing Corporation
LUP	Liberia Unification Party (LUP)
MOJA	Movement for Justice in Africa
NDPL	National Democratic Party of Liberia (NDPL)
NGO	Non-government organisation

NPFL	National Patriotic Front of Liberia
NPRAG	National Patriotic Reconstruction Assembly Government
NRCL	Nimba Redemption Council of Liberia (NRCL)
OAU	Organisation of African Unity
PAL	Progressive Alliance of Liberia
PPP	Progressive People's Party
PRC	People's Redemption Council
PRO	"Public Relations Officer" security system
PTSD	Post-traumatic stress disorder
RUF	Revolutionary United Front
SBU	Small Boys Unit
SMC	Standing Mediation Committee
TRC	Truth and Reconciliation Commission
TWP	True Whig Party
UK	United Kingdom
ULIMO	United Liberation Movement for Democracy
UN	United Nations
UNDP	United Nations Development Program
UNHCR	United Nations High Commission for Refugees
UNOMIL	United Nations Observer Mission in Liberia
UP	Unity Party
US	United States
WHO	World Health Organisation
WMD	Weapons of Mass Destruction

PREFACE

It's been many years since I lived in Liberia, and even longer since I lived in my family's village of Jeadepo.

I was happy and carefree. Like most children, I took my tranquil childhood for granted, assuming things would never change. But life, and the world, intervened.

Though I didn't know it then, my country was as fragile as the little corn dolls I adored. And, in my lifetime, I would witness its brutal destruction.

Along with my people, I would live through unimaginable horrors, whilst those in power tore our beloved country apart from within. Memories of the loved ones we lost and the traumas we suffered will forever torment those of us who survived the atrocities of war.

And yet, before all this chaos, there was calm. And for me, that calm existed about fifty years ago, in a tiny village in south-eastern Liberia.

PROLOGUE

Esther hurried along the deserted road, clutching her shawl closed against the wind that tugged at it. She cast an anxious glance at the sky. It had darkened alarmingly since she left her cousin's house, and she did not like the look of the bluish-green thunderclouds that were rapidly gathering on the horizon.

Just the day before, her brother had sent word from the United States (US) that her travel documents were in order, and he had booked flights for her and her tiny daughter. They would soon begin a new life in the "Home of the Free and the Land of the Brave". Though she trilled with excitement and anticipation, she also felt a little fearful at the prospect of being so far away from home and the people she loved so dearly.

Esther and her cousin Zakel had been close since childhood, and she could not leave without saying goodbye, even though it meant journeying all the way over to the New Kru Town community of Bushrod Island. So, she had left little Rita Bell sleeping peacefully in her grandmother's arms and headed over to spend a few precious hours with Zakel.

They got carried away talking about this and that, paying no heed to passing time or the darkening sky outside. When Esther finally realised how late it was, she hurried out the door, hoping to make it home before the worst of the storm hit.

Another glance at the sky, and she realised she'd left it too late. Fat drops of rain pelted down on her bare head, shoulders, and arms. She sighed – she had no umbrella. Briefly, she considered turning back and waiting out the storm in the warmth of Zakel's house. But she longed to see her little girl, so, resigning herself to a drenching, she put her head down, hunched her shoulders up to her ears and trudged along the muddy path.

Thunder rumbled ominously overhead. Esther jumped as a loud **CRACK** shook the surrounding air. The lightning had been so close that all the hairs on her body stood on end. She felt an odd heat emanating through the chilly rain. A few paces ahead of her, a dead tree burned by the side of the road. The lightning bolt had struck its trunk, causing it to burn. Red-orange flames crackled and spat as they devoured the tree from the inside out. Acrid smoke filled the air. Esther raised her shawl to cover her nose and mouth. Mesmerised by the incongruency of fire and rain coexisting in one place, Esther stared into the flames for a long moment. Eventually, the sensation of wind-whipped rain stinging her skin snapped her out of her reverie. Clucking her tongue at her own foolishness, she pressed on through the storm. *Not far to go now.* She was almost home. Thoughts of her little bundle of joy caused her to quicken her pace.

As she rounded a corner, Esther stopped abruptly.

This section of the street was in chaos. The storm must have been particularly bad here. Tree branches, leaves, and other detritus lay strewn everywhere. She rubbed her eyes to clear phantom images of the burning tree that partially obscured her vision, but even with clear eyes, she could not figure out how she would negotiate the obstacles that had all but blocked her path.

Thunder continued to rumble overhead, and the wind whipped at her scarf. *If only the rain would ease!* Tears pricked the corners of her eyes. Esther summoned up her courage, swallowed hard and began carefully picking her way through the debris. She tried to focus on the ground beneath her feet, taking one shaky step after another. She was almost clear of the worst of it when something cold and metallic slithered from its resting place on the branch of a fallen tree and struck her painfully on the ankle. Esther looked down just in time to see the bare metal end of a fallen power line striking her wet skin. White-hot pain shot through her body. Agony, unlike anything she had ever experienced before, flooded her whole being. A final image of her little girl's angelic face. Then all went dark.

INTRODUCTION

The earliest records of human habitation in the area now known as Liberia date back to the Oldowan Earlier Stone Age some 2.9 million years BP to 1.7 million years ago.

As far back as the twelfth century, Portuguese traders recorded dealings with African tribes, such as the Kissi, Dei, Kru, Gola, and Bassa, that still form part of modern Liberia's richly diverse indigenous population.

Currently numbering around five million people Liberia is home to sixteen ethnic groups, including indigenous tribes (the Bassa, Gio, Kpelle, Grebo, Mandingo, Kru, Mano, Gbandi, Krahn, Vai, Gola, Loma, Bella, and Kissi), Americo-Liberians (descendants of immigrants from the US), descendants of Caribbean immigrants (known as Congo People), and about five thousand persons of European descent.

The Portuguese, Dutch, and British established trading posts in the region that became known as the Pepper Coast, and later, as the Grain Coast for the abundance of melegueta pepper grains it produced.

In 1822, the American Colonisation Society (ACS), believing that people of colour would be better off in Africa, sent volunteers to the Pepper Coast to establish a colony. Tropical diseases killed all but one thousand eight hundred and nineteen of the four thousand and seventy-one emigrants who arrived in Liberia between 1820 and 1843. However, the ships kept coming, and by 1867, thirteen thousand people of colour from the US and the Caribbean had moved into Liberia. These Americo-Liberians and Congo People neither identified nor assimilated with the indigenous native tribes they encountered. Instead, they developed a unique ethnic group, whose culture they infused with American political republicanism and protestant Christianity.

Clashes between the colonial settlers and indigenous tribes, such as the Kru and Grebo, were inevitable, and soon, the Americo-Liberians adopted a system that brought Western religion and education to the indigenous tribes, while simultaneously robbing them of their freedom and binding them to slavery. For example, under Americo-Liberian rule, indigenous tribesmen could not claim citizenship of their own land until 1904.

Liberia declared independence from the ACS on 26 July 1847, issuing its own Declaration of Independence and promulgating a constitution based on the United States Constitution. On 24 August of the same year, Liberians adopted the eleven-striped national flag, and established the Republic of Liberia. Leadership of the fledgling republic was largely in the hands of the Americo-Liberians, who, from the outset, asserted political and economic dominance along the coast, prohibiting foreign trade with tribes in the interior.

The True Whig Party (TWP), made up primarily of Americo-Liberians maintained social, economic, and political dominance of the country for more than a century from Edward James Roye's inauguration in 1870 until Samuel Doe seized power following a bloody military coup in 1980.

PART 1

1970s–1980

PEACE IN THE VILLAGE

The Beginning

I was born in Pleebo in Maryland County and given the name Rita Bell Toe Wleah by parents I would never really know. All I know about my father is that he was the Chief of Aviation at Roberts International Airport, the main airport in Liberia. He left before I was born. And a falling power line tragically electrocuted my mother, Esther, when I was just three months old. Despite these unhappy early experiences, my childhood was humble but happy.

Following my mother's untimely death, they took me to Jeadepo village, where my doting grandparents and loving aunt (my mother's sister) raised me as my mother would have.

So, my early years were happy ones, filled with the affection, compassion, and love of a close-knit family. I always felt cherished, safe, and content.

Rocking my dolls

In the bosom of my family, I grew into a beautiful and charming Liberian girl. My best friend was a girl named Comfort, who had a wonderfully pleasant soul. Occasionally, we would slip down to the creek where we would make up games to play and swim for hours. I treasure the memories of the happy times we spent bathing in the creek with the other children from our village.

One of the games we played was a popular girl's game that involved clapping your hands and doing certain dance steps. Hopscotch was another favourite, as well as various ball games and tag.

Best of all, I loved to play with the dolls I made from palm stalks and corn ears. A new corn husk was a cause for immense excitement. I would spend the afternoon turning the corn strings into plaits, imitating the hairstyles of the local missionaries. I used to "borrow" my grandmother's comb and comb their hair.

These dolls are my children, I thought as I teased apart the delicate white threads trailing from each piece of fresh corn. I adored their thick, shining ponytails, and the way they glittered in the sun. I would pull out the green leaves surrounding the husks and imagine I had dressed each one in a prim new pinafore. To me, the corn dolls looked just like the foreign faces that came every so often to visit my village. My ideal, my hope, was to one day be just like them.

Grandpa did not like me playing with dolls, fearing that this form of play would lead me to give up on my education and become a mother too early in life. So, even though we hardly ever went hungry as a family and could spare the corn, he would take the dolls away, telling me that, "An ear of corn is food and not a toy." I would cry when Grandpa took the corn dolly from me. He would try to distract me by encouraging me to play with palm leaves, twisting them into different shapes that might resemble tiny people. Obediently, I played with the palm people. But they could not replace my little corn dolls with their shiny plaits. I would pout and mutter about this until Grandpa gave in, returned my doll and allowed me to continue my game.

Whether palm or corn, I tried to treat my dolls with the same affection. I would wrap them up in a sling made from a piece of cloth and carry them close to my body, rocking and soothing them in case they ever cried. They didn't, though.

Eventually, their hair would fall out, but that hardly mattered to me. I would cradle each bald baby close, knowing I was its mother. That was enough.

Grandma

I grew up being loved by many people, including my grandparents, sister, uncle, aunties, cousins, and, not forgetting, my affectionate friend Comfort, whose name I love and am proud to mention here. She is a wonderful soul, and she will always remain in my heart.

My grandparents Mary and David were strong and tender in equal measure. Words cannot do justice to the love that they showed us. At night, I would often crawl into bed with them, lying on either of their chests and listening to their breathing as they fell asleep. It felt like the safest place in the world.

My grandma played an especially big role in my life in those early years. She gave me so much hope, and she inspired me to work hard and to excel in life. She was a mentor and role model for me in all aspects of life. My days with her were truly exceptional and priceless. I was her darling girl all the time – even when I made her mad, she would curb her anger and allow love to take over.

There was nothing worth more to me than my grandma's love. My greatest fear was losing her, and every night in my prayers, I asked God to give Grandma the grace to live forever.

Whenever my grandma talked to me, she was very positive and attentive. She taught me to believe in God and to understand that He is the God of miracles. She told us He is faithful and provides all our needs. So, I must not despise my humble beginnings, but believe in God, believe in His word, and stand on the promises He made concerning my life. She also told me how important it is to believe in myself if I wanted to succeed in life.

Now, I pass this message on to my children and to others who come to me for counsel. Life will always have challenges, that is a fact. But with faith in God, and in yourself, you can move mountains – no matter how large or high they might be.

I was so blessed to have a sweet, adorable, and loving grandma, filled with so much positive energy, which she showered on me. Her influence in my life continues to this day.

My grandma also taught me practical skills, such as how to behave properly with good manners, how to cook, how to take care of a family, how to treat my future husband and how to run a household.

Whenever Grandma was preparing a meal, she would have me sit beside her and show me how it was done. When I was old enough, she let me help by doing small things, until eventually, I could cook on my own.

She gave me every single thing I needed, and God blessed our home. He always made provision for my grandparents.

Dreams of being a farmer

Experiencing not a single day of hatred or wrath in those early years, I thrived in the love and affection of my warm and compassionate family. We all shared a single home, and it was a place of comfort and pleasant dreams. Life was beautiful.

The whole family would gather round at night, arranging our seats in a circle and listening intently while my grandparents told us amazing stories. Many of them were traditional stories that imparted important truths about Liberian culture and values, significant family relationships, histories of our cultural origin, moral mentorship, and other important lessons that at once fascinated and educated us. Our family never tired of hearing these beautiful tales, and we still feel their impact on our lives today.

At the conclusion of each enlightenment story, Grandma would ask us about our ambitions for the future.

"What do you want to be when you grow up?" she would ask, and we would respond with magnificent and ambitious answers.

"A doctor."

"A lawyer."

"A civil engineer."

"A journalist."

Someone even said, "President of Liberia." But all I wanted was to be a farmer.

I also planned to marry a farmer and to have many children. Day and night, this dream of becoming a farmer played out in my head, until I could not hide my desire to follow my farming dream any longer. So, one night, I came out with it and told my grandma I wanted to be a farmer. She said nothing, only gently laughed and shook her head. I wondered what I had said that was so funny. *Perhaps she had not heard properly, or misunderstood me?* I opened my mouth to explain, but Grandma held up a finger to stop me and said, "Oh my dear, you do not know what you are saying." Then she stunned me by adding, "God has blessed you with travelling grace. You will travel from country to country in your lifetime, and you will eventually live in a white race country."

I was speechless, wondering how she knew this, and how such a wild prophecy could ever come to fulfilment. Recalling how close my mother and I had come to living in the US, I thought perhaps Grandma meant I might end up there after all.

Though she continued to remind me of her prediction for my future, every time we met, with tremendous passion and conviction, Grandma's prophecy did nothing to subdue my love of farming, and my desire to be a farmer one day. My fondest memories are of those carefree days, living and working on the farm.

During the terrible years of civil war, I forgot all about this prediction, and it wasn't until 1996, when I left for the United Kingdom (UK), that I realised Grandma had been right after all.

The gilded age

While I remained wrapped up in the bosom of my family, content with life in my little village, my country Liberia likewise enjoyed a period of relative peace and prosperity.

President William Tubman had been in power since 1944 (before I was born). Known by many as the 'father of modern Liberia', Tubman was the longest serving president of Liberia, remaining in power until his death in 1971.

During his time in office, Liberia experienced a period of prosperity, growth, and modernisation. So much so that, in the 1950s, the country achieved the second-highest rate of economic growth in the world, and from 1950 to 1960, Liberia experienced an average annual growth of eleven-point-five percent.

Tubman claimed to be "committed to the concept of a free enterprise system, democracy, and a pragmatic search for solutions to problems of multinational existence."

"We envisage a synthesis composed of individual states retaining their own way of life, but united by mutual exchanges of peoples, goods, and ideas, by pacts of non-aggression, non-interference in the internal affairs of other states, and of perpetual peace," he said.

He encouraged foreign investment and garnered revenues for the government to construct and modernise infrastructure. During Tubman's tenure, to encourage trade, he transformed the Port of Monrovia into a free port with paved streets, hospitals, and a public sanitation system. In 1948, Tubman also launched a literacy program across the country.

Whereas previously the country's economy had relied almost entirely on rubber, modernisation made it possible to diversify the economy to include iron, coffee, palm oil, sugar cane, and rice. The Tubman government oversaw the construction of several thousand kilometres of roads, and a railway line to connect the iron mines to the coast for export.

Concessionary companies, such as the Bong Mining Company, the Liberian American Swedish Mining Company (LAMCO) in Yekepa Nimba County, Mano River Mining Company, and the Liberia Produce Marketing Corporation (LPMC) flourished.

By the time Tubman died in 1971, Liberia was the third-largest exporter of iron ore in the world and had the world's largest rubber industry. The country had attracted more than one billion US dollars in foreign investment and boasted the largest mercantile fleet in the world.

During this gilded era, Liberia also played a key role in international affairs. It was a founding member of the League of Nations and the United Nations (UN), a vocal critic of South Africa's system of apartheid, a proponent of African independence from European colonial powers, and an advocate of Pan-Africanism. Liberia also provided funding for the Organisation of African Unity (OAU).

School

My favourite memories of the years I spent growing up in the village were of the times I spent working and playing on the farm.

Each morning, I would get up before five to walk the long distance to the creek, bringing the water back balanced precariously on my head. Then, before heading off to school, I would crush rice by hand, so that it was ready to cook with the vegetables for our evening meal. I loved farm life immensely, and my desire to be a farmer was unwavering and all-consuming.

As much as I loved and adored everything about my life on the farm, I absolutely *hated* school so much that I would get angry whenever the topic of school came up.

My grandparents were adamant that I should get a formal education, and they enrolled me in the village mission school. I was equally adamant that I had no need for school since I wanted to become a farmer and, in time, also marry a farmer.

Unaware that my grandparents could see further into the future than I could and were trying to give me the best possible chance in life by ensuring that I was well educated, I railed against their insistence that I go to school. But they were my guardians, and I had to obey them. So, I dragged myself to school even though I despised school and everything to do with it.

To make matters worse, on school days, I had to walk long distances from my grandparents' farm to school and back. This was especially hard when I was tired and hungry after a long day at school.

I felt restless all the time at school. Being bound to my desk frustrated me. I struggled in lessons and found it boring having to read, write and do sums. I've always preferred doing more practical things, working with my hands.

Geography held some fascination for me, as I enjoyed learning all about other countries and cultures, and the prospect of getting to travel one day thrilled me.

I also liked sports. Mostly because it required using

your hands and feet rather than your head. Kickball was my favourite, along with running, and track and field.

God's blessings

Now that I am fully grown, I realise how important it is for children to be educated, so that they are prepared for the future. And I often think about how much easier my life might have been if I had had a formal education.

However, I do not regret my lack of education. God has empowered me with a powerful intellect that has made it possible for me to learn many skills, such as how to use the computer. These skills have helped me to adapt and survive in many settings, including the modern city of London in England.

He has also gifted me with skilled hands and strength of character that helps me to earn a living and make a positive impact on the lives of others.

My desire to see unprivileged children getting quality education prompted me to contribute to the provision of quality education to many children in my native country. And I continue to do so through my humanitarian programs and donations.

A new calling

As I grew older, my plans for the future changed. Rather than being a farmer, I decided I wanted to be a nurse. This was much more than just a childish dream. My grandma was the village midwife, and after I had seen firsthand how she attended to women in labour, I decided this was my calling.

Whenever I assisted my grandma, I would talk to the women and comfort them. I stroked their hands as they cried, groaned and heaved – their faces damp with tears and their legs shiny with dark red blood.

If a woman found it hard to push, Grandma would send me to fetch the leaves of a certain plant. We squeezed the juice from these leaves onto the woman's tongue to induce labour. Both mother and baby would come through the experience happy and healthy. With no squeamishness at all, I cut the umbilical cord with a blade. I took pride in this task. No woman ever died on my grandma's watch. It was inspiring. I wanted to be just like her.

I loved the strange, sheltered world of the birthing room. I felt completely safe there. No men were allowed to enter. Although, even if permitted, they would not have come. The men in our village preferred to spend their time sitting in the sun, cheerfully drinking palm wine.

Womanhood

The golden years of childhood passed quickly. Before long, my aunt was showing me how to tie a piece of absorbent cloth, called a lappa, around my waist each month when I menstruated. There were no disposable pads in those days. So, the lappa had to be washed after every use.

Though it had the rather unpleasant name of

"woman's sickness", we saw the onset of menstruation as a rite of passage into womanhood. Whenever it happened, they excused me from helping with the cooking, as my hands were considered unclean. But, unlike many other girls, my monthly cycle didn't cause me pain. I just felt excited that I was now a woman.

Carefree teenage years

My teenage years were the best of my life. I spent the days playing, dancing and enjoying life on the farm and in the village. It felt good to be surrounded by the love of my peaceful, close-knit community.

Love is one of the most important things in life – it inspires us, heals us, motivates us and gives us a reason to live each day – even when times get tough. To have love for others and for yourself is to have a priceless treasure that no one can take away.

Without love, it is impossible to achieve your dreams. You need inspiration to figure out your dreams, motivation to work towards your dreams, and strength to sustain you through the trials and tribulations you face while chasing your dreams. Following your dreams brings purpose and meaning into your life. And dreams help you create a place for love in your life – so the cycle completes itself.

In the absence of love, hate takes over. Love and hate cannot dwell in the same environment. They cannot coexist. They are contrary to one another and can never harmonise. Hate affects our lives negatively. The language of hate is condemnation, slander, lies, and flattery.

Hate never appreciates the differences between people. Instead, it limits our tolerance, distorts our belief systems, and provokes animosity. It invariably leads to destruction.

The atmosphere of love in my grandparents' home was clear to all who entered, and their behaviour modelled the definition of true love. Because of that foundation, I never stopped caring for people – no matter how bad things got in my life.

Hide-and-seek

As young teens, we often played hide-and-seek at night. Usually, it was the girls against the boys. Whatever group was supposed to hide headed for their hiding places, and after ten to twenty seconds, the group that was supposed to seek went to look for them. Once we had found everyone, we'd switch sides, and the game would begin again. It was very exciting for us to play this game at night – especially since we did not have access to modern technology like TV, movies, and video games for night-time entertainment.

Most of the time, young girls and boys used the occasion to meet their crushes. We did not get to see our boyfriends and girlfriends all the time. So, the game gave us an excuse to spend a few stolen moments alone in the dark together.

Young love

At sixteen, I fell head over heels in love with a young man from our village. We had been good friends throughout our childhood, and as teenagers, we fell "in love" with all the passion and intensity of the very young. But we kept our relationship a secret because I was underaged, and we both still lived with our parents. Only my best friend Comfort knew about us.

When I was in the village, my favourite pastime was dancing. I was an excellent dancer. We would ask the boys to beat the samba, and while they kept the beat, all the girls would show off their talents. We would take turns, dancing one at a time, each person displaying her own style. The dancing would go on and on all night.

When it was my turn, I was always very excited. Even before I started to dance, everyone would chant my name, and because of that, I never wanted to stop. Sometimes, my boyfriend would watch me, and he would be like, "Wow!" And I would feel so proud.

An unexpected pregnancy

Though there was a lot of fun in our village, it was also a place of great morality. We did not live in whatever way we pleased. There were clear social norms and traditions that everyone followed and obeyed. As a result, there was order, unity, and peace in the village.

So, when I realised I was pregnant, I was both mortified and terrified. Being so young, my boyfriend and

I had little experience of life, and we did not know how our parents would react. Convinced that we would be in hot water, we tried to hide the pregnancy. But, after a few months, this became impossible. My grandparents noticed my symptoms and saw how my appearance had changed. It did not take them long to realise what was going on, and our secret came out.

To our great relief, the reaction we received was not one of anger as we had expected. My grandparents only wanted to know who the father of the baby was. A young girl falling pregnant could cause fights between families when it was unclear who fathered the child. But when I told them who it was, they approached his family, and everyone agreed he was indeed the baby's father. So, at least there were no disagreements over the paternity of the child.

When my uncle Bennie arrived from Monrovia, announcing that I was to come and live with him, it devastated me. I cried bitterly as I realised that my life in the village was over. *How could I live my life without my grandparents? What would I do without the support of our close-knit community?*

I was heartbroken. I still clung to my dream of being a farmer's wife and a mother of many children. I adored my boyfriend, and all I wanted was to raise a family with him in our village.

My boyfriend's family had other plans. They wanted him to stay in school and get a good education. So, to prevent us from making the same mistake again, they sent him to Bong Mine to pursue his studies there.

"But we're in love," I protested with tears in my eyes. Our parents were unmoved.

"You're too young to understand right now," they said. "But one day, you'll see this is all for the best."

No amount of crying or begging would sway them. They knew that, as teens, we were not mature enough to shoulder the responsibility of a child. They did their best to support and protect us. And, being brought up as I had been in a family that followed strict social norms in these matters, I could not go against Uncle Bennie's wishes. So, in the end, my boyfriend ended up in Bong Mine, and I went to Gardnersville to live with my uncle Bennie. Except for the two of us, everyone in our families was happy with this arrangement. And as predicted, years later, I finally understood that our parents had done what was best.

It was very hard for me to leave my village, my grandma, and her beautiful stories, my friends, and our sweet games. After all, I had spent my childhood in the village surrounded by their love and supported by the affection I received from my grandparents and everyone else in the village. But my family could not afford to keep me and my child, whereas Uncle Bennie was well off, having an important position in the United Nations High Commission for Refugees (UNHCR).

Fortunately, I was young, and before long, I grew excited by the thought of living in the capital. So, when the time came for me to say my goodbyes, a mixture of pain and anticipation swirled through me. I tried to appear strong, putting on a brave face and smiling through my tears as I bid farewell to friends and family.

I was sixteen, and, although I did not know it then, I would never see my village or my grandparents ever again.

Dark clouds gather

While my idyllic teenage life came crashing down around me, my beloved Liberia was undergoing a major crisis that I was barely aware of.

William Tubman had been president of Liberia for twenty-seven-years. During this time, he attempted (through his policy of national unification) to reduce the social and political differences between his fellow Americo-Liberians and the indigenous Liberian population. However, the gap between the "Country People" (Indigenous Liberians) and the "Congo People" (Americo-Liberians) remained wide.

While Tubman's "Open Door" economic policy brought a great deal of foreign investment into the country, it also deepened the divide between wealthy Americo-Liberians and the rest of the population.

Most of the development that occurred under the Tubman regime focussed on building infrastructure in Central Monrovia and in Tubman's hometown of Harper. While only a few miles away, many people lived without access to running water, schools, or basic facilities.

When President Tubman died in hospital in 1971, Vice President William R. Tolbert took over the reins.

When, in 1972, Tolbert gave his inaugural address in Kpelle, he became the first Liberian leader in the nation's hundred-and-twenty-five-year history to address the people in an indigenous tongue.

Tolbert's early years in power resonated with promise. He introduced liberal reforms and supported the cause of lifting common Liberians out of poverty, introducing initiatives such as "Rally Time", "Mat to Mattress", and "Total Involvement for Higher Heights".

One of Tolbert's first actions as president was to dismantle Tubman's "Public Relations Officer" (PRO) security system that had seen family members reporting each other to the security services for even the slightest of perceived disloyalties to the Tubman regime.

He also attempted to address economic disparities between Americo-Liberians and indigenous ethnic tribes by ushering in reforms that gave indigenous Liberians rights and freedoms that denied them until that point. Tolbert endeavoured to make university more accessible to a broader spectrum of Liberians and invested in low-cost housing schemes, such as the Stephen A. Tolbert Estate, Old and New Matadi Estates, the E. Jonathan Goodridge Estate, and the Amilcar Cabral Estate.

Working with Agrimeco, an Israeli-managed government entity, the Tolbert regime introduced large-scale projects to increase the production of rice, palm oil, and other crops, and encouraged modernisation of the agricultural sector.

Not all Tolbert's actions were as noble, however. Though he remained in power until his assassination on 12 April 1980, political dissent increased during his tenure as a growing number of factions vied for control of the nation's wealth. In the end, the civil wars that ensued would cripple our once thriving country, crushing the economic prosperity of Liberia's golden age.

Sovereignty and independence

The rise in the black power movement during Tolbert's presidency led to unprecedented numbers of indigenous Liberians achieving higher levels of education. Seeing that other African nations were running their own affairs, these educated people likewise sought to take control of their country. As a result, two major opposition movements sprang up, both eager to seize control from the Tolbert government.

In 1973, Dr Amos Sawyer co-founded the Movement for Justice in Africa (MOJA), and in 1975, Gabriel Baccus Matthews became founding chair of the Progressive Alliance of Liberia (PAL). Later, the PAL would form the unwavering and formidable political party known as the Progressive People's Party (PPP), which would become the face of indigenous Liberians and present a strong opposition to Samuel Doe's regime.

Introducing a two-party system

President Tolbert responded to the changing political climate by initiating socially liberal reforms, including cutting tuition by half at the University of Liberia, in order to make tertiary education more accessible, and attempting to remove Americo-Liberian symbols, such as Matilda Newport Day, from the country's calendar.

In February 1978, he transformed Liberia's political system from the one-party system that had been in place since 1877 into a two-party system that recognised the Progressive People's Party (PPP), headed by Gabriel Baccus Matthews, as the legitimate opposition party to the ruling TWP. Sadly, the dream of a two-party system in which the electorate had a free choice did not last long.

Novel approach to foreign policy

Tolbert took a significant new direction in the country's foreign policy. Deviating from the old pattern of traditional unipolar ties to the West, he established new multi-polar relationships with countries, such as Algeria, China, Cuba, Czechoslovakia, and Russia. He also renegotiated foreign investment terms to benefit the nation.

Tolbert sought to stress Liberian sovereignty and political independence and pledged stricter regulation of foreign businesses operating in Liberia.

He worked to strengthen ties with neighbouring countries through initiatives such as the 1973 Mano River Union Agreement between Liberia, Sierra Leone, Guinea, and, later, Côte d'Ivoire. The agreement was intended to foster greater unity, solidarity, and cooperation between member states and a peaceful coexistence amongst these nations. By promoting peace, security, democratic principles, and the pursuit of good governance, it aimed to reinforce regional integration and development, integrate commerce and industry, create employment, and enhance social and cultural affairs.

Disillusionment and dissent

Sadly, despite its early promise, the Tolbert regime was marred by economic troubles and growing tensions between Americo-Liberians and indigenous Liberians. Ultimately, this resulted in instability across the country.

Dissatisfaction over several government economic policies culminated in outrage at the massive amounts of money spent hosting the 1979 OAU Summit that plunged the already shaky economy further into debt.

Traditionalist members of the TWP, along with some members of Tolbert's cabinet, strongly opposed his initiative to appoint indigenous Liberians into government positions, viewing this as an attempt to usurp their positions.

In the end, much of Tolbert's good work was undone when he resorted to the old TWP tactics of suppressing opposition by any means necessary, including harassment, intimidation, arrests on false charges, issuing life sentences and executing anyone suspected of disloyalty. Tolbert was also accused of using corruption and political nepotism to retain power.

THOUGH YOU SLAY ME

The Rice Riots

The tipping point came in early April 1979, when Minister of Agriculture Florence Chenoweth proposed an increase in the price of rice. The price of the country's principal commodity and staple food jumped from twenty-two dollars per bag to twenty-six dollars per bag overnight. Tolbert's government justified the price increase by saying that the move would bolster the struggling agricultural sector. Ostensibly, a higher price per bag would make farming more lucrative and encourage farmers to stay on their land, rather than migrating to the rubber plantations and cities in order to make money.

These noble intentions did little to placate the average person who could not afford the exorbitant prices. A public outcry against the price hike ensued. Political opponents accused Chenoweth and Tolbert of feathering their own nests at the expense of the ordinary people. It was not lost on the public that the price increase would directly benefit the pair as their families operated large rice farms and would therefore garner a tidy profit from it.

On 14 April 1979, what started out as a peaceful protest led by the PAL descended into chaos. Two thousand PAL activists, who purported to be non-political, and merely providing a voice for the under-served masses, staged the protest. However, it quickly degenerated into a riot when over ten thousand rebels (the so-called "backstreet boys") joined the march. The rioting mob looted hundreds of businesses, causing over forty million dollars' worth of damage to property.

Tolbert responded by importing seven hundred troops from Guinea to reinforce the police force and ordering them to open fire on the demonstrators. Accounts vary, placing the number of demonstrators killed between forty and seventy, with around five hundred people injured in the riots.

In his 2008 testimony to the Liberian Truth and Reconciliation Commission, D. Kaine Carlo, former General Coordinator of the People's Redemption Council, testified that hundreds of PAL members had been arrested and approximately three hundred killed during the crackdown.

Shockwaves from these events rippled across Liberia. Tolbert's reputation lay in tatters, and widespread disillusionment gave rise to mass rioting, disorder, and violence throughout the country.

In what would be Tolbert's final attempt to appease the country's increasingly disillusioned and frustrated indigenous population, he officially recognised the legitimacy of the PAL's political party, the PPP, in January 1980. The move had little effect on the situation. Unrest continued to mount across the country, and in March of the same year, Tolbert reversed his decision, placing a ban on the PAL and rearresting Gabriel Baccus Matthews and the rest of the organisation's leadership.

The assassination of Tolbert and the rise of Samuel Doe

The crisis came to a head on 12 April 1980 when a group of armed men under the leadership of Master Sergeant Samuel Doe of Grand Gedeh County staged a vicious military coup, killing twenty-six of Tolbert's men and assassinating President Tolbert. The coup marked the end of the Whig regime and, with it, one hundred and thirty-three years of Americo-Liberian political domination.

Doe installed himself as the first indigenous Liberian head of state, declared martial law and suspended the constitution. He formed a military regime known as the People's Redemption Council (PRC), comprising himself and the seventeen soldiers who had aided in the coup. Gabriel Baccus Matthews became the new Minister of Foreign Affairs, and Councillor Chea Job Cheapoo was appointed Chief Justice.

Upon taking control, Doe issued orders for the immediate release of political prisoners and activists sympathetic to his cause, including approximately fifty vanga leaders of the PPP.

Hundreds of arrests and mass executions of former government officials marked the early days of Doe's presidency. On 22 April 1980, he held a hasty pseudo trial in which thirteen of Tolbert's cabinet members faced charges of high treason, gross violations of human rights and rampant corruption. A guilty verdict followed, and they were all stripped naked and marched through the streets of

Monrovia before being publicly executed by firing squad.

Notwithstanding these violent acts, many Liberians welcomed Doe's regime as he claimed to be seeking equal rights for all Liberians and promised a new system of governance and social organisation that would support the country's common people.

Currying favour with the US

During his first years in office, President Doe quickly ingratiated himself with the US by openly supporting its Cold War foreign policy in Africa and severing ties with Libya and the Soviet Union. He set Liberia up as an asset to the US in the cold war by granting US Rapid Deployment Forces staging rights on twenty-four-hour notice at Liberian sea- and airports. In so doing, he convinced then US President Ronald Reagan to more than triple Liberia's foreign aid. Doe opened Liberian ports to US, Canadian, and European merchant ships, which led to significant foreign investment from shipping companies, and Liberia became known as a tax haven.

PART 2

1980

GARDNERSVILLE

Uncle Bennie

My Uncle Bennie Debblay was the most prominent member of our family. Well educated and blessed with a lucrative job, he brought home a handsome salary. This made Uncle Bennie the most successful person in our family, and, according to our African culture, it also made him responsible for taking care of the rest of the family. Some "breadwinners", as we called these successful people, viewed this responsibility as a burden, but my uncle saw it as a pleasure.

Bennie was a truly good man – always loving and supportive. Despite his notable achievements, he had a spirit of genuine humility and compassion. He was always there for our family, and we were forever grateful to have such an exceptional person looking after us.

The house in Gardnersville

Uncle Bennie's house stood on one acre of land that included several three-bed bungalows for visiting relatives to stay in. Besides being home to his children, Uncle Bennie's seven-bedroom house was also a place of refuge for any members of our family who fell on hard times and needed help. We all came to him, and he never disappointed us or turned anyone away. Nor did he ever tire of helping those less fortunate than himself. People from all over, most especially relatives, but also others, sought refuge in his home. He welcomed them with open arms and gave whatever help he could, be it financial or otherwise.

When I moved into my uncle's house in Gardnersville at the age of sixteen, it did not take me long to realise that this was the ideal place for me to make a new start. I embraced this opportunity with open arms. The high walls and enormous gates made me feel like I was entering my private kingdom every time I went through them.

A warm welcome

God had blessed Bennie with five biological children and four stepchildren. He was married to a lovely woman named Caroline, who clearly cherished him above all others. Not only that – she welcomed every relative of his into their home.

On the day that I arrived, I received an overwhelming reception from Caroline and their kids.

THOUGH YOU SLAY ME

Everyone was eager to meet me, and the warmth of their welcome overwhelmed me. They immediately ushered me off to the girls' room – a dormitory-style room, where we all slept in bunk beds. We spent our evenings chatting and gossiping, telling each other stories, and watching television together. Uncle Bennie's girls became far more than cousins to me – we were like sisters. There was a lot of hugging and talking in my life during that time, and there still is. I've always felt that talking about feelings is important, and that's probably where it all started.

Homesickness

Although I enjoyed the company of my cousins and received a lot of love and support from Uncle Bennie and his wife, I often wept secretly from homesickness in those first few months in Monrovia.

Memories of the precious moments filled with beauty and peace that I had known in my village life came flooding back as I lay in the dark. I recalled the pieces of chicken I used to wrap in leaves for my grandparents to eat, and the games I used to play out in the yard with pieces of chalk and stones. My thoughts would drift to all the lovely people who had showered me with tenderness – those dear ones who had danced with me in my joys and held me when I cried.

I thought of my grandparents sleeping in their bed with the space between them I had occupied as a child now forever empty. I missed my grandma most of all. Every day,

I would think about her and long to be back by her side. I often wished I could go back to that simple existence, even though I knew it was impossible.

One day, I asked my uncle whether he had a picture of my mother as I had always longed to have one. She died when I was just three months old, so I had no memories of her. I wanted to have some image of the woman who brought me into this world. I thought her image might comfort me and assuage the loneliness and homesickness I felt.

But my uncle said it was not yet appropriate for me to look upon an image of my mother. This bewildered me. "Why not?" I asked.

He replied, "According to our African tradition, you cannot have access to this picture, nor can you see it."

Puzzled by his vague answer, I asked again, "But why not?"

But he only said, in a voice that told me this was his final word on the matter, "You must wait until you reach a certain age. Then you may see your mother's image." This troubled me, though I had no choice but to back down and be satisfied with his reply.

Still, I longed for the comfort of my mother. So, every night when I lay in bed, I prayed that my mother would reveal herself to me. Sadly, she never did, and in the end, I never got to see a photo of my mother because all the photos my uncle had of her got lost in the upheaval of the civil war.

THOUGH YOU SLAY ME

Christopher

I gave birth to my first son, Chris, at the Duside Hospital in Firestone District, Margibi County, where my uncle Joseph worked. We returned home amidst an outpouring of love and support from my whole family. Everyone helped to take care of Chris in those early days, most especially my uncle Bennie and his darling wife.

Shortly after he was born, Caroline and Bennie told me that the family had decided it was best for Chris to be raised by my sister Diana. Being separated from my darling boy devastated me, but once again, I had very little say in the matter. So, I gave him up to my sister, and it would be a very long time before I saw my son again.

School in Monrovia

Uncle Bennie feared that my entry into motherhood at such an early age would prevent me from living up to my full potential. He believed I was destined for greatness and was keen to see me succeed. So, all the time I lived with them in Gardnersville, he and Caroline encouraged me to continue with my education.

School in Monrovia proved to be an even bigger challenge than it had been in the village. They enrolled me in a private Catholic school in Monrovia – a far cry from our little village school. My uncle paid a large amount of money for me to attend this fancy school, and I *hated* it. I cried every morning and begged not to be sent to school.

My uncle and aunt pleaded with me to consider my future, but I found it hard to concentrate at school, and I was convinced that I would never understand the subjects they tried to teach me there.

There were some aspects of school that I liked. For instance, I didn't mind being trooped out for a parade on Flag Day (24 August) or Independence Day (26 July), and I enjoyed playing sports, such as kickball – a mixture of baseball and soccer in which one person throws a soccer ball to another who kicks it and then tries to run the bases. But I hated being stuck in a classroom all day.

To make matters worse, at Uncle Bennie's house, school didn't end once we left the classroom. Oh no! When we got home, there were tutors already waiting for us. Their job was to make sure we did our homework. I tried to dodge them. Being good at hide-and-seek, I would find imaginative spots to hide from them. But they always found me and dragged me back to my books.

Despite my rebellion against formal education, my desire to go into nursing grew stronger as I became inspired by Caroline, who was a nurse at the JFK Hospital. I often recalled the happy days spent rocking and tending to my corn husk children and helping my grandma to take care of the women in our village. There had been a separate missionary hospital close to my house in the village, and sometimes, I daydreamed of going back and working there as a nurse. I thought I would gladly do all my old chores, like sweeping the floors and fetching water in the mornings, if only I could go back and live in the village with my grandparents again.

THOUGH YOU SLAY ME

A harmonious life

Uncle Bennie set an excellent example for us to follow through with his humble and generous lifestyle. Although my uncle and aunt worked long hours, they still had time for their family. We all sat around the dining room table to have family conversations, during which I learned family values, civilisation, the significance of social compatibility, and above all, how to show genuine love for others. Caroline, in particular, was a very loving mother to us all, and I still call her Mum to this day.

Our lifestyle was based on Biblical principles, and they brought us up with strict moral and spiritual discipline, tempered with unconditional love and affection. On Sundays, we would dress up and head to church, where we would listen to the singing, praying, and preaching – sometimes joining in, but often just listening. The services were three hours long, but I always enjoyed them. God was important to me, and He still is.

There was no room for disunity or hard feelings in Bennie's house. So, we all lived in harmony, and as a result, I have many happy memories of the time I spent there.

I stayed with Uncle Bennie in Gardnersville until the civil war broke out.

Part 3

1980–1985

TROUBLE BREWING

Tense times

When Samuel Doe took control of Liberia in 1980, he received some initial support from a variety of indigenous Liberian ethnic groups, who had been denied political influence in the country since 1847. However, any hopes that Doe would improve the plight of indigenous Liberians were quickly quashed when, fuelled by his concern over a counter coup, he clamped down on anyone who appeared to oppose him.

Echoing the actions of the very government he had sought to overthrow, Doe subdued all perceived or actual opposition to his leadership through violence and intimidation, causing many of his critics to flee the country in fear of their lives.

Tension escalated when Doe became convinced that his leadership was being threatened from within his own party. This fear rapidly devolved into paranoia, and within one year of taking over, he executed his vice head of state and comrade-in-arms Thomas Weh Syen along with four other PRC members, accusing them of plotting against him.

Targeting the Gio and Mano ethnic groups in particular, he systematically removed people of other ethnic groups from the PRC, replacing them with individuals from his own Krahn tribe and forming a Krahn-dominated government. Doe's preferential treatment of the Krahn ethnic and mistreatment of other groups lead to heightened tension in Liberia, setting the scene for hostilities.

1985 Election

Echoing the sentiments of many Liberians, certain influential politicians, including Madam Ellen Johnson Sirleaf, Dr Amos C. Sawyer, and the Hon. Gabriel Baccus Mathew, pressured Samuel Doe to legitimise his claim to power through democratic means. In 1983, Doe responded by issuing a new draft constitution providing for a multi-party republic. He held a referendum the following year in which the new constitution was approved.

Doe dissolved the PRC and took up the role of President of the Interim National Assembly on 26 July 1984. He lifted the ban on political parties and staged a presidential election on 15 October 1985. Four parties contested the elections: Doe's National Democratic Party of Liberia (NDPL), the Liberian Action Party (LAP), the Unity Party (UP) and the Liberia Unification Party (LUP).

Official figures showed a victory for Doe with 51%

of the vote. Doe's NDPL won twenty-one of the twenty-six Senate seats and fifty-one of sixty-four seats in the House of Representatives.

However, the validity of the results was strongly contested – not in the least because Samuel Doe allegedly stationed members of the Armed Forces of Liberia (AFL) around the electoral commissioner's compound and would not allow anyone to leave until they had announced the results – a move which smacked of intimidation. It was also alleged that Doe had the ballots taken to a secret location where members of his own hand-picked staff counted them.

In the end, Doe declared his victory, and the electoral commission left Liberia post-haste after the announcement. Rumour had it Doe had paid them vast sums of money to throw the election in his favour.

Although the US ultimately endorsed the results, many foreign and local observers believed the election was heavily rigged, and that LAP leader Jackson Doe had, in fact, been the victor.

The Quiwonkpa coup

General Thomas Quiwonkpa, a member of the Gio (Dan) ethnic from Nimba County, joined the AFL at the age of sixteen. He assisted Samuel Doe in the April 1980 coup to overthrow the Tolbert regime. In mid-May of the same year, Quiwonkpa was appointed major general and leader of the new AFL. Two months later, he was promoted to brigadier general. However, he soon fell into disfavour, and in 1983, he was demoted and charged with attempting to overthrow the Doe government.

In November 1983, he joined other influential members of the PRC, most notably Charles Taylor (head of the general service agency) and Prince Yormie Johnson (aide to Quiwonkpa), who sought refuge from Doe's monopolised control across the borders. All three would eventually challenge Doe for leadership of the country.

Two years later, on 12 November 1985, less than a month after the general election that saw Doe take over the presidency, Thomas Quiwonkpa, accompanied by a small group of heavily armed men, entered Nimba County from Sierra Leone. Their objective being to stage a coup that would topple the Doe regime. Doe's troops soon suppressed the ill-fated mission. They captured and killed Quiwonkpa three days later. Krahn soldiers mutilated his body (some reports claim that parts of it were cannibalised) and put it on public display in Monrovia.

Samuel Doe's already corrupt and totalitarian government responded by increasing oppression of its own citizens (especially those from Nimba County) in ever more aggressive and inhumane ways.

Newspapers were shut down, and political activity banned. A curfew came into effect, with radio and television stations announcing that anyone caught in the streets after six in the evening would be considered a rebel and executed immediately.

In his campaign of retribution, Doe also launched

a vicious strike against the Gio (Dan) and Mano ethnic groups in Nimba County, killing an estimated three thousand people. During one such action, Doe's men arrested many people, including three hundred Nimba children (ranging from seven years to infants) and brought them into Schieffelin, where they massacred them and dumped their bodies into a mass grave.

These actions further inflamed the ethnic rivalries that had been simmering since Doe took power and set the stage for Charles Taylor to step in and incite a rebellion that would throw the country into civil war.

Doe's inauguration

Doe was inaugurated with great pomp and ceremony as the twenty-first president of Liberia on 6 January 1986. This event legitimised Doe as President in the eyes of the world at large, and the Doe regime became the official governing body of Liberia. However, most of the elected opposition candidates refused to accept their seats.

Immediately after his inauguration, Doe launched several campaigns to curry favour with the West. Claiming that he wanted to reduce the risk of further depression, dislocation, and the potential collapse of the Liberian economy, he petitioned the International Monetary Fund, the World Bank, and the European Community to send money managers to assist with proposed reforms to the government's spending habits.

To further show off his new image, Doe released individuals charged with complicity in the abortive Quiwonkpa coup and called for national reconciliation amongst his political opponents.

Although Doe had garnered substantial support from the US government in the first five years following his rise to power in 1980, it did not take long for US diplomats to become frustrated by his actions. His decision to run for the presidency especially rankled as he had led the US to believe that he intended to bow out of politics once the elections had been scheduled. And they were further aggrieved by reports of widespread irregularities in the election process.

Yet, despite these misgivings, the Reagan administration continued to support Doe – albeit to a lesser extent than before – instructing him to stamp out corruption, stand by his proposed financial reforms and offload unprofitable state enterprises. They supported his requests for money managers at the International Monetary Fund, World Bank, and European Community to supervise Liberian tax collection and government spending. The US government applauded Doe's release of political prisoners, insisting that he tolerate political opposition or risk losing US economic aid.

PART 4

1989–1992

THE WAR BEGINS

Charles Taylor attacks

In 1989, former Liberian politician Charles Taylor, who had been removed from President Samuel Doe's cabinet and, subsequently, imprisoned for embezzlement, escaped and fled to Libya. There he trained as a guerrilla fighter. In December that same year, he returned to Liberia as the leader of an Ivory-Coast-and-Libyan-backed rebel group, calling themselves the National Patriotic Front of Liberia (NPFL).

On 24 December 1989, Taylor and the NPFL mounted an insurgency from neighbouring Cote d'Ivoire into the border town of Butuo in Nimba County. Their objective being to overthrow the Doe government and instate Taylor as head of the country.

Taylor's forces garnered plenty of support in Nimba County, where thousands of Gio (Dan) and Mano ethnic people had suffered persecution at the hands of President

Doe's armed forces. This led to a rapid expansion of NPFL troops from a few hundred to a vast army.

As they moved through the county, NPFL rebels killed border officials, soldiers from the AFL, government officials, and Mandingo men whom they accused of being informers. In one incident, in the town of Tiaplay, the rebels allegedly entered a mosque and killed seven Mandingo men at prayer.

In response to Taylor's attack, President Doe launched a series of ruthless counterattacks, sending two AFL battalions to Nimba between December 1989 and January 1990. AFL soldiers reportedly killed Gio (Dan) and Mano civilians indiscriminately, burnt down villages, and sexually abused women and children.

In an incident in the town of Cocopa, AFL soldiers shot and killed members of the Gio (Dan) and Mano communities for having fed rebel troops passing through the area. In reprisal, the rebels killed several Mandingo and Krahn working on a rubber plantation in the area.

These brutal attacks and counterattacks sparked a vicious inter-ethnic civil war with appalling human rights violations on all sides. Within four months, Liberia was thrown into a state of turmoil. The heinous acts of terror and brutality her people experienced led *Africa Watch* monitors to describe the situation as nothing less than a "human rights disaster".

Food as an instrument of war

As the clash between NPFL rebels and AFL soldiers spread across the country, non-combatants became both collateral damage and intended targets. The rebels targeted the Krahn ethnic, while the AFL considered the Gio (Dan) and Mano tribes to be traitors and enemies of the state. Both sides tortured, killed and displaced thousands of civilians and burned villages. The preferred modus operandi was to attack the village, ransack the houses, steal property, kill the villagers, then burn the village and any adjacent agricultural land to the ground.

Such guerrilla warfare and scorched earth tactics employed by both sides took a heavy toll on the already shaky agricultural sector, causing a nation-wide food shortage. Taylor, in particular, is alleged to have used food and water shortages to his advantage, threatening to cut off food supplies if people did not join his cause.

Taylor's child soldiers reportedly refused to let villagers harvest their crops and deliberately contaminated drinking water by throwing corpses into streams and wells.

Rebel factions, lacking central supply stores, also suffered under the shortages and resorted to looting and pillaging necessities. These so-called "food" or "clothes" attacks were nothing more than organised raids carried out on unarmed civilians. Taylor not only tolerated this behaviour but also allegedly encouraged it, ordering his soldiers to collect rice and meat from the villages they captured.

The rebels saw no need to restrict themselves to taking the necessities. They also allegedly helped themselves to anything that took their fancy, including sentimental items such as wedding albums. They tortured and killed anyone who objected to them taking whatever they liked, butchering any chiefs or villagers who could not provide them with food, cattle, goats, or sheep.

Wealthier villagers were abducted and held to ransom, while others were arrested on the flimsiest of charges and jailed until substantial amounts of money were paid for their release.

These atrocities resulted in the displacement of approximately half of Liberia's population during 1990. The combination of forced displacement, starvation, and dehydration led to the deaths of thousands of innocent Liberians because of malnutrition and disease.

Appeals for international aid

The Doe government rapidly lost control of the country. The rising state of anarchy and faction leaders' seizure of certain key areas compelled President Doe to make an appeal for international aid.

Notably though, rather than appealing to the Economic Community of West African States (ECOWAS) itself, he first approached the Nigerian military ruler General Ibrahim Babangida and President Eyadema of Togo. This move revealed both a lack of confidence in ECOWAS and his close friendship with Babangida.

Between January and May 1990, hundreds of thousands of Liberians fled the country to escape the violence. This mass influx of refugees into neighbouring countries became a cause for concern amongst West African heads of state who soon joined President Doe in making several appeals to the US and the UN to help resolve the conflict.

The US, however, declined to provide military aid – in part because its own struggles in the aftermath of the Cold War largely overshadowed the troubles in Liberia.

Looking to the OAU for guidance, Liberia eventually garnered some support from newly appointed AOU chair President Yoweir Museveni of Uganda who, along with Secretary General Salim Ahmed Salim, agreed to waive the AOU norm of non-intervention, citing the unusual character of the Liberian crisis. Plans were put in place to negotiate a ceasefire. Sadly, this would be years in the making, and in the meantime, the blood of innocent Liberians would continue to be spilled.

General Babangida

The AOU appointed General Babangida to lead a regional force into Liberia within the framework of ECOWAS. Babangida seized the opportunity, not only to exercise statesmanship but also to divert national and international attention away from mounting socio-economic problems and political abuses in his own country.

He invited the ECOWAS heads of state to a

meeting in Banjul in The Gambia on 30 May 1990 to discuss his plans for the establishment of a Standing Mediation Committee (SMC) that would settle disputes and conflicts within Liberia.

Believing that subduing the uprising in Liberia would be a simple matter of bolstering police presence in the country, the US applauded the formation of a West African peacekeeping force, declaring it to be an outstanding example of an 'African solution to an African problem'. Meanwhile, a war, far more savage than they realised, raged on.

By May 1990, rebel troops had driven the AFL back as far as the town of Gbarnga, and by the end of the month, the NPFL, having amassed ten thousand troops, had captured the coastal town of Buchanan. Subsequently, the rebels easily wrested control of Gbarnga from the fractured AFL contingent, leaving Taylor's rebel forces in control of most of the country, except for Monrovia. The NPFL directed its troops toward that city.

NPFL splits

By June 1990, the rebels had advanced to within five miles of Monrovia, and panic spread throughout the capital. There were shortages of everything. Looting was commonplace, and the AFL had degenerated into anarchy with soldiers raping, pillaging, and killing people indiscriminately.

During the siege of Monrovia by NPFL forces,

Charles Taylor fell into a leadership dispute with Prince Johnson, one of his supporters. A member of the Gio (Dan) tribe, Johnson soon set up a splinter rebel faction, which he called the Independent National Patriotic Front of Liberia (INPFL).

Johnson's men captured the Monrovia suburbs of Bushrod Island and Caldwell and set up a military base in Caldwell.

The NPFL and INPFL continued to hold AFL-controlled Monrovia under siege until one fateful day in July 1990, when they pressed their advantage on the already crippled city. I was there to witness the devastation of this attack firsthand.

Caught in the crossfire

While staying in Gardnersville with Uncle Bennie, I had a friend named Mamie. She was the daughter of former senator James Chleeh. We had grown close over the years, and since she lived nearby, I often visited her in her home.

It was during one of these visits in July 1990, while my friend and I were rubbing minds and having some fun at her place, that a sudden and powerful blast shook the house. We ran outside to see what was going on. To our horror, we discovered we were right in the middle of a war zone.

The battle for control of Monrovia was raging all around us. Heavy gunfire and mortar blasts roared through the streets of Gardnersville as AFL troops violently resisted the NPFL and INPFL rebels attempting to overthrow this last outpost of the Doe government.

I have never been so terrified in all my life. For a moment, we were all too stunned to move. We stood there bewildered until a fresh barrage of firing burst forth, and we all began running for our lives.

With no order to our flight, we ran hither and thither, trying to get away from the fighting, which seemed to come from everywhere all at once. There were people everywhere, and in the turmoil, I became separated from Mamie. I never saw her again.

My heart beat hard in my chest, and I covered my ears with sweaty palms as I zigzagged through the rubble that only moments before had been the orderly streets around my friend's home. Before my eyes, the once lovely city of Monrovia was torn apart, leaving behind nothing but utter devastation. I tried not to look at the dead bodies that lined the streets, their open eyes staring up at an unforgiving sky.

Blood, dust, and the stench of human fear hung thick in the air as I scurried through the ruins. Everywhere I went, I encountered more fighting. I kept low to the ground as bullets zipped by, breaking stone and shards of brick and glass off nearby buildings and ripping through the bodies of the unfortunate souls around me. Neither the army nor the rebels had any scruples over killing innocent civilians.

THOUGH YOU SLAY ME

I tried to make my way back home, running down one alley and then another, but the fighting blocked all passage through the city. Tears streamed down my cheeks as I ran, etching their tracks into the pale dust that coated my face and arms. I was all alone. Mamie and my family, if they were still alive, were beyond my reach.

Finally, overcome by despair, I sank down on the stone floor of an alleyway. I crouched with my head in my hands and sobbed. How I longed to just curl up on the rough stone and give in to the weariness that dragged at my limbs! But people's screams and renewed gunfire prompted me to move on.

I knuckled back my tears, took a deep breath, summonsed all my courage and stood up on shaking legs. I peered out into the street. People were running helter-skelter, trying to get away from the gunfire. Which way should I go? I had to find somewhere where I would be safe until I could find my family. But where?

Many people hid in churches and other buildings around the city, hoping to find sanctuary there. But I could not bring myself to join them. I wanted to get as far away from the guns as possible. I noticed a group of people heading toward Bong County, and having few other options, I joined them.

Later, when I learned about the tragic fate of the displaced people who had chosen shelter over flight, I thanked God that He had spared me and led me out of the war zone. Hundreds of innocent men, women, and children sheltering in buildings all around the city precinct were brutally massacred.

The Monrovian Church Massacre

The most infamous of these killings took place in St Peter's Lutheran Church in the Monrovian district of Sinkor. Known as The Monrovia Church Massacre, it is considered the worst single atrocity to have occurred in the bloodbath that was the first Liberian civil war.

The massacre began on 29 July 1990 when thirty AFL soldiers, mostly from the Krahn ethnic group, scrambled over the church wall. Showing complete disregard for the sanctity of the church, these soldiers entered the building and opened fire on the refugees sleeping on the church floor. They ran through the entire building, killing people as they went. They even went upstairs and executed people sheltering in the classrooms. With no time to flee, the people lay flat on the floor. But the soldiers merely walked up to them and shot them where they lay. Those who tried to escape, including women who fled with babies strapped to their backs, were gunned down from behind. Others were hacked to death.

Two Grebo women begged for mercy and, though they were spared, the soldiers slashed them and forced them to hide beneath the corpses, saying that they (the soldiers) had to spill blood from everybody that night.

Only a handful of adults and children survived the massacre. Some, like the Grebo women, survived because of their ethnicity; others hid under the corpses of their loved ones. The survivors remained hidden until the following day when a Guinean doctor came to the site. She heard a baby crying and, as she picked her way through the corpses to find and comfort the crying baby, the traumatised survivors slipped out of their gruesome hiding places and made their presence known.

Exodus from Monrovia

The rebel advance on Monrovia caused widespread panic and anarchy throughout the city. NPFL soldiers confiscated food, money, and other goods from civilians, even dressing up as women to gain entry into people's homes. Once inside, they demanded food, forced residents to cook for them and helped themselves to anything they wanted. Any resistance was met with brute force.

AFL soldiers likewise demanded money and food from civilians, killing anyone who tried to stand in their way. Not to be outdone, the INPFL fighters made similar demands, assaulting people who would (or could) not pay them.

As with my family, many Liberian families became separated, with mothers, sisters, brothers, and fathers fleeing in different directions. And many people, both male and female, were abducted. Far too many of us have never seen our loved ones again.

Over time, hunger and disease took hold, causing so much death and destruction that Monrovians were forced to flee en masse. In the aftermath, Freedom House accurately described our beloved city of Monrovia as "a virtual ghost town of starving people and rotting corpses".

On the road to Bong County

Even as we fled the war, we remained harassed and persecuted. Militia forces detained us again and again, committing so many atrocities that the road we followed became lined with corpses. Never in my life had I ever witnessed such misery and destruction. There was so much blood and suffering, I could hardly bear it.

In order to hang onto a shred of sanity amidst all the horror, I tried to recall the love and affection of my family. It brought tears to my eyes as I pictured their dear faces. Through the heartache and desolation, we trudged ever onward. The road seemed as unending as our suffering.

Every couple of miles, we would come to a roadblock erected by the rebels. Dead bodies lay piled up around the gates — a warning to anyone who thought they could escape.

Terror filled our hearts as we waited in line to be questioned by the soldiers. They grabbed anyone they believed might belong to the Krahn or Mano tribes and tortured them, cutting off arms, legs, and heads.

In the villages and at the checkpoints, soldiers from all three warring factions committed similar acts of cruelty, singling people out at random, torturing and killing them in the streets. They forced some people to stare at the sun until they became blind and made others watch while they tortured and raped their wives and daughters before murdering them.

A favourite torture technique, known as tabay, involved tying the person's hands behind their back so tightly that their chest pushes forward. Sometimes the chest cavity breaks open under the strain. The soldiers loved to stab the victim in the chest with a bayonet and watch their chests explode.

From time to time, a group of rebels would find a pregnant woman. Then they would pull her out of the line and place bets on the sex of her unborn baby. As the woman struggled and screamed, the rebels would slice open her belly and remove the child to reveal the sex. Those who won would cheer and clap. When the fun was over, they would behead the woman and leave her body on the side of the road.

When I got to the front of the queue at the checkpoint, a surly rebel soldier demanded, "What tribe are you?"

My mouth was so dry from fear, I could hardly speak, but I croaked, "I am a Grebo girl."

Unimpressed, the rebel soldier said, "If you are a Grebo, say something in your language."

Fortunately for me, I could speak my dialect, and so I did, and they allowed me to pass through. Many other civilians in our group could not speak the language of the tribes they claimed to be from, and the soldiers shot them dead in front of us, leaving the bodies to litter the road.

Many people who joined us on our journey had fled from their villages to escape the fighting, often after their friends and families had been tortured and killed in front of them, and their homes destroyed. People related horrific stories of how their friends and relatives had suffered at the hands of the fighters.

"They accused my father of being a Doe supporter," one woman said, "and cut his head off with a power saw, right in front of us. As punishment for our complicity, they burned my brother with plastic, broke my sister's fingers, and stabbed me in the stomach with a bayonet."

It seemed these people had harassed and abused every one of us. They took everything, looted and burnt down homes, and left us with nothing – not even our dignity. Stories of torture, mutilation, rapes, beatings, and all forms of cruelty were common. Some people had experienced psychological torture, such as being forced to sing, dance, and cheer while the fighters raped, tortured or killed their loved ones.

"They made the townspeople sing and cheer while they forced my father to drink dirty water," another woman told us. "Then they told him to dance while they forced my brothers and sisters to strip naked. They shot my father many times before cutting my brothers and sisters to pieces with cutlasses."

The soldiers burned down homes, forcing people to march long distances (forty miles or more) to get away from the violence, just as we were doing. Desperate to reach a place of safety where we could find some peace, we walked night and day, with only brief periods of rest. After a while, the young children and older people amongst us floundered. Food and water were scarce. Sobbing mothers were forced to abandon their infants on the side of the road because there was no more milk to feed them. Many people dropped dead from hunger, illness, or exhaustion along the way. I felt as though the world was crumbling around me; my heart was breaking with every step. But, in the midst of these circumstances, I trusted the Lord. I kept praying that He would protect me and my family and see us through these troubled times.

Adam and Eve Creek

We took respite from our long journey at Cuttington University campus in Suakoko District in Bong County. Having suffered heavy losses and unspeakable hardships on our journey, we arrived, exhausted, bloody, and half-starved. Without hesitating, we all headed to a nearby creek to rest and bathe.

We made a dismal sight – so many travel-weary people stretched out on the bank hungry, crying, scared and in pain. One or two had been pushing elderly relatives in wheelbarrows for miles and were only too glad to put their burdens down and rest their weary backs, arms, and legs.

We called the river Adam and Eve Creek because everyone there undressed at the same time and waded into the water to bathe, without bothering to separate men from women. We were simply too tired and traumatised to care about age, gender, or anything else.

As I stripped off, however, I realised my period had arrived. I flushed with embarrassment. I could not believe it. Why now? I longed to join the others in the creek and wash away the dirt and grime of the road. But now I was unclean, and besides, I did not want to be seen with blood running down my legs. So, I kept myself apart from the crowd and sat alone on the bank. Misery overtook me, and I sobbed into my hands.

Though I did not know it then, an old lady had been watching me and noticed my distress. She ambled over to me. I wanted to run away and hide, but she smiled kindly at me.

"My name is Ma Fanta Fofana," she said. "What is yours?"

I told her my name, and she smiled even wider than before. Then she surprised me by taking off her lappa and holding it out to me. "Here," she said. "Take it. It's yours." A wave of gratitude washed over me. I had no idea how she knew of my dilemma, but I took the cloth gratefully.

"Thank you, thank you, thank you," I said. Then I headed off to find a quiet spot further downstream where I could wash and freshen up. When I finished, I walked back up to join the group. Ma Fanta saw me coming. She hurried over to me and wrapped me in a warm embrace, as though I were her very own daughter. I felt the tears pricking my eyes again, but I swallowed them back down as Ma Fanta showered me with her cheery presence and warm affection. She wanted to know all about me and my family. So, we spent that night and the following two days together in Cuttington, sharing stories and getting to know one another. I told her I was from Jeadepo and had been living in Monrovia when the war came. She said she was from Gbatala village in Bong County.

Life in Cuttington

Our time in Cuttington went by in a haze. Food and shelter were scarce. We were fearful, uncertain, and miserable. But, most of all, we were hungry. We spent almost all of our time trying to find food and a reasonably soft and safe patch of ground to sleep on. I also frantically searched for news of my family.

Meanwhile, the battle for control of Monrovia raged on, and the world fell further into chaos. Liberia is a small country, and with so much of it in the hands of rebel factions, it became difficult to find a safe place to stay. So many groups were fighting over the same small piece of territory, and one could never be certain from one day to the next which groups controlled which areas. If you strayed into the wrong area, you would pay for your mistake with your life. So, we were compelled to stay constantly on the move.

The INPFL, led by Prince Johnson, was notorious for shooting first and asking questions later (more like never). If an area was under their control, you knew to keep yourself scarce because the INPFL would kill you if they saw you.

The soldiers looted homes and set them on fire, so there was no guarantee of a roof over your head, utensils to eat with, or somewhere to take a shower. We lived amongst the ruins of destroyed buildings, amidst the constant rattle of gunfire – sometimes in the distance, other times terrifyingly close. I slept outside and bathed in streams or rivers with other displaced people, rinsing and ringing out my clothes on the bank. We used the pages of books as plates to balance our meagre portions of rice and sweet potato leaves.

The situation became so dangerous that even going out to find food and water was risky. You might go out to a market one day and have no one harass you, but the next day, they would stop you at a checkpoint that wasn't there yesterday. As the war went on, these checkpoints sprang up everywhere, and the soldiers manning them were ruthless men who would not think twice about shooting you if they suspected you of being part of the Krahn or Mandingo ethnic groups – even if you were just a civilian.

I was usually the one who had to make the trips to look for food because, although my Grebo ethnicity put me closer to the Krahn than the rebels' Gio (Dan) and Mandé ethnic groups, I spoke English. And, since they did not consider English the language of the enemy, I rarely found myself on the wrong side of the soldiers.

The threat of being executed remained very real though, and it was only hunger and love of my friends and family that pushed me out the door. Each time I went, my heart pounded like a drum in my ears, my mouth felt dry as dust, and my palms were sweaty with fear.

We did not dare send children out on the streets. They snatched boys up and sent them to camps where they forced them to become child soldiers. Girls faced a far worse fate — they forced even the young ones to serve as sex slaves. The soldiers raped and murdered many of them in cold blood.

One day, while I was out looking for food, I heard screams and a commotion up ahead. Four soldiers had seized a girl of about nine years old. They formed a circle around her, blocking my path. I kept my distance, trying to shrink back against the wall so they would not see me. Knowing what was coming, I tried to look away, but my eyes were drawn back to the tableau unfolding in broad daylight on the street.

One soldier held the girl, while another punched her in the belly. His blow winded her, and she doubled over. The soldier holding her let her limp form drop to the ground like a sack of potatoes. She lay in the dirt, moaning and clutching her stomach. The soldiers hurled insults at her, spat on her, and kicked her repeatedly. The one who had punched her held his rifle to her forehead, preventing her from getting up. Then they stripped the clothes from her tiny body and held her down, while, one by one, they raped her – right in front of me. I longed to run away from the scene, but fear kept me pinned to the spot. Even the slightest movement might alert them to my presence.

When they had all had a turn, they shot the poor girl in the head. I pressed my hand over my mouth to stifle a scream. Silent tears flowed down my face. I was helpless to do anything to save the girl. All I could do was stand there, trying to look away, but transfixed by the horror of it all. She was one of many girls violated and murdered right in front of us. The memories I have of those assaults haunt me to this day.

Food became increasingly scarce, and I did not know to what to do. We were starving; we had no money, and the little we had was worth nothing. I walked the streets hoping to beg some food from someone, but everyone seemed to be as poor and hungry as I was. Finally, I sat down on the steps of a burnt-out building and wept. I don't know how long I sat there, my head buried in my arms, but after a while, a soldier's voice stirred me from my grief. "What are you doing here, woman?" he demanded. "Don't you know you can't loiter around this district?"

"I – I'm sorry," I stammered, hastily getting to my feet and turning towards home, trying to hide my tear-stained face from him as I did so.

"Wait," he called after me. I stopped dead in my tracks, too scared to move a muscle. *This is it,* I thought.

I'm going to be raped and murdered in the street. My heart was beating so loud I could barely hear what he said next. "You hungry?"

It took a moment for me to register that his tone was almost friendly, or at least not hostile. I turned to face him but kept my eyes downcast. "Yes," I said, my voice just above a whisper. Part of me wanted to run and hide, sure this was some kind of trap. But hunger won out, and I stayed put.

"Why don't you come with me, then?" His voice still carried the honeyed tones of earlier, but I sensed an undertone of steel in them that made me shiver. It was clear, although he was asking, that he expected me to obey. *What could I do?* With no idea of where we were going or what would happen when we got there, I followed him down an alleyway. We had not gone far when the alley ended abruptly in a pile of rubble. Two neighbouring buildings leaned against each other like a pair of drunks heading home in the early hours. They blocked out the sun, creating a dark alcove where the man ordered me to take off my clothes. I saw the glint of lust in his eyes. When I refused to do as I was told, he struck me. "Do you want food or not, you stupid woman?" My belly rumbled loudly in reply. He laughed. Then his face became stern once more. "So, what are you waiting for? I haven't got all day. Take off your clothes and let's get on with it."

I had heard rumours that getting any form of food in those days involved doing sexual favours for men, but

I had scarcely dared to believe that I would ever do such a thing. Yet, I was starving, and though it revolted me, I was terrified that the soldier might change his mind and shoot me instead. So, I did what he asked of me. When he finished, he ordered me to put my clothes back on. I did so with the greatest of relief. Then he fished in his backpack and gave me a hunk of stale bread, some cheese, and a few apples. Disgusted by my actions, but also exuberant at being able to bring food home for the others, I hurried away. This would not be the last time I gave up my body for a few morsels of food. In those dark times, we all did what we had to do to survive.

On the road again

As the fighting intensified, it became impossible to stay in Cuttington. Besides, I had not been able to garner any news about my family in the few days we spent there. So, I told Ma Fanta that I planned to resume my journey to Gbarnga, the capital city of Bong County, where I hoped to locate some members of my family or at least find someone who knew of them. Without a moment's hesitation, Ma Fanta said she would accompany me.

The next day, we gathered our meagre possessions and headed off on foot as part of a large group of people making their way to Gbarnga.

As before, our journey was arduous and fraught with danger. We walked until our feet and legs ached. We slept fitfully on the side of the road or wherever we could find shelter. The militia groups continued to hound us, murdering our fellow travellers on the grounds of real or imagined offences we had little knowledge or understanding of. No one was safe. The militia could take any little thing as a sign that you belonged to the enemy tribes. Some rebels said they could identify a Krahn or Mano simply by the way they smelled. They executed people right in front of us because they "smelled like an AFL soldier".

If you wore the wrong colour clothes or had any marks on your body, either side might target you. If you had scars or marks on your legs, the rebels said they were obviously from army boots, and they executed you for being a soldier. Gunshot wounds also marked you for death. If someone looked too healthy or too wealthy, they accused them of being government fat cats, who ate up the country's resources.

They construed marks on the forehead as signs that you were a Mandingo because, being Muslims, they prostrated themselves daily in prayer. When the soldiers saw people with these marks, they tortured and killed or, if female, took them as bush wives.

The AFL were no better, killing innocent people for having the wrong type of tattoo or wearing red clothes or denim pants (taken as a rebel uniform), or being too slow to flee from certain areas (a clear sign, according to the soldiers, that you intended to resist them).

Ma Fanta Fofana saves my life – twice

It was on that long and terrible walk that I saw true love and courage in action. My dear friend and travelling companion Ma Fanta Fofana turned out to be one of the bravest people I have ever met, and I am forever in her debt for saving my life – not once, but twice on that journey.

The first time was at the very first checkpoint after we left Cuttington. A rebel soldier pulled me away from the group. His grip felt like iron around my upper arm. To my horror, I took in the wild look in his eyes, the knife in his free hand, and the massive AK-47 assault rifle slung over his shoulder. I knew better than to struggle, but my knees gave in, and I stumbled as he pulled me along.

"Get up," he commanded.

"Please," I begged from my kneeling position on the ground at his feet. "Please, don't hurt me." His reply was a kick in the stomach. I fell forward, winded. I tasted dirt in my mouth. It stuck to my wet cheeks and grated between my teeth.

"Get up or I will kick you again." I struggled to my feet, my breath rasping through my raw throat. "Now come with me, and I'll show you what we do to women like you." He grabbed me by the neck and pushed me over to where a pile of dead bodies lay like sandbags against a wall.

"Please, you don't have to—" I was sobbing now.

"Shut up, woman." He lifted the knife to my face, pressing the point of his blade against the skin below my right eyeball. "Shut up and move or I will cut you."

I closed my eyes and let him lead me towards the pile of bodies. But before we had taken more than two or three steps, we halted. I opened my eyes, and to my surprise, there stood Ma Fanta Fofana. "What do you want, old woman?" the soldier demanded.

Ma Fanta sank down onto her rickety old knees at the soldier's feet and pleaded with him to release me. At first, he ignored her, telling her roughly to go away and mind her own business, but she insisted I was her daughter, and that he was not to harm me. The man did not understand Ma Fanta's words because she was speaking in her own dialect, but by this time, we were attracting some attention. Another soldier came over and translated Ma Fanta's words.

I do not know what they said, but the soldier who had assaulted me suddenly let go of me. He pushed me away from him, so hard that I fell backwards and landed awkwardly on the ground. Then he stalked away, looking furious. I sat where I had fallen, rubbing my bruises as tears of relief rolled down my dust-coated cheeks. Ma Fanta came and sat beside me. She put an arm around me and told me funny and inspiring stories until my sobs subsided. Then we got up and rejoined the slow-moving group.

The second time Ma Fanta came to my rescue was just outside Gbarnga. We were passing a line of soldiers when one called out, "Hey, you with the red lappa." I had Ma Fanta's red lappa draped over my shoulder, so I looked around, praying that he hadn't meant me. His evil grin was all I needed to tell me I was, in fact, his target. "Come here," he beckoned. He had a gun cradled in his arms, so I reluctantly obeyed.

Since that first checkpoint, Ma Fanta had not let me out of her sight. She had been walking right beside me and saw what was happening. Before I made any move towards the man with the gun, this brave old woman pushed past me. She ran up to the man and once again knelt before him, begging for him not to hurt me. "She is my daughter," she told him. "Please, show mercy to an old woman and don't take my only child from me," she pleaded. Her loud cries and wailing attracted a lot of unwanted attention – not only from the crowd but also from some of the military officers. The soldier looked crestfallen, but decided not to risk the displeasure of his superiors and wisely allowed us to pass.

Gbarnga

When we reached Gbarnga, we were foot-sore, tired and hungry. People in the group were milling about, unsure of what to do or where to go. I was exhausted and utterly devastated by everything that had happened to me, and to my fellow Liberians, over the past weeks.

A pall of bitter sadness and despair came over me as Ma Fanta took me into her warm embrace one final time. "We must go our separate ways now, my dear," she said. "But remember, you will always be my daughter. You are mine forever, my child, and from now on, Gbatala is your home. Promise me you won't forget us. That you will come and visit us in Gbatala when all this is over." As tears flowed freely down both our faces, I made a solemn vow that I would one day build a house in Gbatala and make it my home. It took many years, but I did eventually keep this promise to Ma Fanta.

Ornekel

I cried for a long time after Ma Fanta left. I had been crying for so long that my eyes were swollen, and my face was red and raw from it. I clung to my faith in God like a drowning man will cling to a straw. It was all I had left. The war had taken everything else from me. So, while I cried, I also prayed a silent prayer that God would send someone to help me. And He did.

One of our fellow travellers was a woman named Ornekel. She saw me standing, lost and alone and crying, amid the milling crowd, and came over to me.

"Hey," she said in a gentle voice as she threaded an arm through mine and guided me to a quiet spot where we could sit down and talk. I sank down on the grass, thankful for her calming presence and for the relief of finally being off my aching feet. When we had made ourselves comfortable, and I had got my sobbing under control a little, she said, "I'm Ornekel. What's your name?" I told her, and she immediately asked where I was from.

"I'm a Grebo girl," I replied, adding, "I was living with my uncle and his family in Gardnersville before the trouble started."

"Do you have any friends or family here in Gbarnga? Anyone you can stay with?"

I just stared into my lap and shook my head, fresh tears choking me up.

She put an arm around my shoulders and said, "Don't cry. You can come and stay with me. My family lives here, and we'd be happy to have you."

"Thank you," I replied, taking her hand in both of mine. This time, my cheeks were wet with tears of gratitude. So, Ornekel took me to her father's house. Her family welcomed me in and took care of me.

Ornekel and I shared a room like sisters, and we did everything together. Her family became my new family. They were very generous to me, and we looked out for each other through the turmoil of the first civil war.

Life was far from easy, though. NPFL rebels occupied the entire city of Gbarnga, and we had to be vigilant at all times to ensure our safety. Although we were fortunate enough to avoid any harassment or intimidation from the NPFL and its associates during our time in Gbarnga, I could not stop thinking about Chris and about my family. I longed to be reunited with them again. My heart bled every day for the terrible situation we were in. Weeping was a way of life for me in those days.

Caldwell

On 20 July 1990, Prince Johnson's INPFL arrived in the Monrovian suburb of Caldwell. There, they became engaged in an intense battle against AFL troops led by Brigadier General Charles Julu. The battle raged on for hours. In the end, Prince Johnson and his men emerged as the victors, capturing Caldwell and setting up their base in the area. The INPFL would continue to operate out of Caldwell until Johnson surrendered the base to the ECOWAS Ceasefire Monitoring Group (ECOMOG) in 1992.

Diplomacy fails

In August 1990, while I was in Gbarnga, the politicians were trying, unsuccessfully, to settle things diplomatically.

The SMC, which comprised representatives from The Gambia, Ghana, Mali, Nigeria, and Togo, met and prepared a peace plan, aiming to establish an immediate ceasefire and to deploy ECOMOG troops to ensure that all groups complied with the ceasefire. The SMC also planned to establish an interim administration in Monrovia, pending the ECOMOG-monitored election of a substantive government.

According to official reports of the ministerial conference, substantial disagreements arose between SMC members and the warring parties, particularly over the desirability and timing of a ceasefire; the desirability and composition of an interim government; and the usefulness of deploying a regional peacekeeping force. Their inability to come to any sort of agreement on these key elements of the proposed peace plan eventually led to the breakdown of talks between ECOWAS and Liberia's warring factions.

Because of his stubborn refusal to accept anything less than the unconditional resignation of Samuel Doe, the SMC contemptuously viewed rebel leader Charles Taylor as the principal reason for failing to arrive at a peaceful resolution to the crisis at the Banjul meeting.

For many observers, it came as no surprise that diplomacy failed to produce a resolution, given the constituent members of the SMC – all of whom were military rulers rather than diplomats. However, it was how ECOWAS reacted to this initial failure to negotiate a ceasefire that resulted in uncontrolled mayhem in Liberia.

As political scientist and expert in African politics Professor Clement E. Adibe put it, "Viewed from the perspective of diplomacy, the ECOWAS Peace Plan was a recipe for disaster in Liberia. Very little negotiation took place between members of the SMC and the factions in Liberia, particularly the NPFL whose leader Charles Taylor accused ECOWAS of handing down a set of instructions for him to roll back his forces from Monrovia."

Defiant and agitated, Taylor pointed to the fact that the NPFL had taken up arms, got rid of Doe, and occupied over ninety-five percent of the country. In his eyes, this had earned them the right to rule. ECOWAS accused Taylor of being "arrogantly intransigent" and announced that it would continue with its Liberian initiative, with or without the support of the militia.

ECOMOG forces enter Liberia

Perhaps revealing an inherent lack of confidence in the diplomatic process, ECOWAS moved quickly, and by August 1990, they had the green light from the SMC to establish and deploy ECOMOG as the principal instrument for implementing their Liberian Peace Plan.

The first batch of four thousand West African ECOMOG peacekeepers, led by Ghana and Nigeria, comprised military contingents from the SMC member states, as well as Guinea, Gambia, and Sierra Leone. The force commander had the power to use military operations to monitor the ceasefire. Their aim was to re-establish law and order and create suitable conditions to hold free and fair elections.

Under the command of Ghanaian General Arnold Quainoo, ECOMOG troops landed in the Freeport of Monrovia on 24 August 1990. While Prince Johnson and his INPFL welcomed ECOMOG, Taylor's NPFL and Doe's AFL viewed them as a US proxy force that would jeopardise their chances of seizing control over the country by installing an interim government. As a result, the NPFL, in particular, resisted the deployment of ECOMOG forces in Monrovia, greeting the ECOMOG troops with gunfire and brutal attacks as soon as they set foot on Liberian soil.

A bloody battle ensued, with heavy losses suffered by all sides and many civilians killed in the fighting. ECOMOG finally pushed the NPFL militia back to the outskirts of Monrovia. However, this resulted in several undesirable consequences. It escalated the conflict by pitting the supposed peacekeeping forces against the NPFL warring faction. It diminished the presence and power of the NPFL, and it disrupted the correlation of forces in the local area.

By dislodging the NPFL from their long-held positions, ECOMOG arbitrarily enhanced the position of the rival INPFL militia group, and the latter took full advantage of this situation.

In the last week of August 1990, ECOWAS held a conference of Liberian exiles in The Gambia, aiming to elect an interim government. Faced with very vocal opposition from the warring factions, they elected Dr Amos Sawyer, an exiled Marxist professor at the University of Liberia, to head the interim government in Monrovia – a step which served only to inflame opposition to the ECOWAS plan.

Even the embattled President Samuel Doe accused the ECOWAS leadership of "meddling in Liberia's internal affairs". The NPFL contended that "the ECOWAS discussion of an interim government showed complete and total disregard for the constitution and sovereignty of Liberia" and warned that "if there was any attempt at peacekeeping from any part of the world, [the NPFL] would not allow that force to enter". This set the stage for a military showdown between ECOWAS and the Liberian militia factions.

The Dukuly Prophecy

Mother Wilhelmina Bryant Dukuly was a powerful woman of God. Known as Mother Dukuly, she warned Samuel K. Doe that the Lord was unhappy with his presidential strategy and the decisions his government was making. She cautioned him that there would be consequences if he did not change his ways, predicting in her prophecy that a war would overthrow the Doe regime and result in his death. Given Doe's attitude towards any hint of criticism or opposition, these were very bold statements indeed. Yet Mother Dukuly spoke openly and without fear. When the prophecy came to his attention, Doe immediately ordered the arrest of Mother Dukuly and incarcerated her in Buchanan City Grand Bassa County. There Doe loyalist soldiers brutally tortured, raped, and abused her until she died. In the end, the unrepentant Doe suffered the agonising death that Mother Dukuly foretold.

Assassination of Samuel K. Doe

General Quainoo, Head of ECOMOG, invited Samuel K. Doe to the ECOMOG headquarters in the Free Port of Maher on 9 September 1990. Shortly before Doe arrived, a weaker Gambian contingent of guards replaced the fully equipped and well-armed Nigerian guards stationed around the base. With his safety assured ahead of the meeting, Doe's convoy was only lightly armed, and he left his guards and aides outside as he entered Quainoo's office. While Doe met with Quainoo, Prince Johnson and a group of heavily armed INPFL rebels entered the compound. These men easily overpowered the guards and began executing the members of Doe's convoy – at first individually, and later, in groups. Doe heard the gunshots and expressed his concern. However, Quainoo reassured him that all was well. A short while later, General Quainoo and Captain Coker, the head of Quainoo's Gambian contingent, excused themselves, and, realising the situation, they quickly took cover. By this time, Johnson's men had entered the building. They shot Doe in the leg and executed the rest of his guards.

By the time Johnson's men withdrew, they had captured Doe and massacred more than eighty of his men. ECOMOG suffered no losses during the raid.

They took Doe to Johnson's military base in Caldwell. Johnson had him shackled and ordered his men to cut off Doe's ears to prove that he (Doe) was not protected by any form of black magic. The INPFL soldiers tortured Doe for twelve hours before murdering him and mutilating his corpse. A video recording of the incident, subsequently aired on news bulletins across Liberia, shows Prince Johnson drinking a beer while his men tortured Doe.

They paraded Doe's naked, mutilated corpse through the streets of Monrovia. Some accounts say that they buried Doe's body in a mass grave. However, according to testimony given by Prince Johnson at the Truth and Reconciliation Commission (TRC) Thematic and Institutional Public Hearing in 2008, the body was burnt, and the ashes thrown into a river.

ECOMOG appoints Dogonyaro

Because of its apparent complicity in Doe's assassination and several other deadly encounters with Liberian factions, ECOMOG could no longer be seen as an impartial arbiter, but rather as a faction in the conflict.

To restore its prestige as a credible military force, ECOMOG forces were strengthened to the level of an effective fighting army. General Babangida, Flight Lieutenant Jerry Rawlings of Ghana, and ECOMOG agreed to double ground forces from three thousand five hundred to seven thousand soldiers and reorganise them into a modern fighting force comprising army, navy, and air force.

The more aggressive General Joshua Dogonyaro replaced Nigerian Force Commander General Quainoo. Dogonyaro was immediately tasked with strictly enforcing a complete arms embargo on militant forces in Liberia who refused to subscribe to a ceasefire.

Operation Liberty

With Doe out of the way, ECOMOG focussed its efforts on the NPFL that, by this point, had become entrenched in some of Monrovia's western suburbs. In October 1990, General Dogonyaro united the INPFL and the AFL with ECOMOG and launched Operation Liberty — a ruthless campaign that drove NPFL militia forces out of Monrovia.

In doing so, Dogonyaro freed Monrovia from direct

armed conflict. But, by the time the campaign ended in November 1990, Dogonyaro's "limited offensive" had caused so much collateral damage that many individuals and organisations, including Western diplomats who had initially been sympathisers of ECOMOG, issued frantic calls for the general's removal.

Operation Liberty resulted in weeks of fighting, which destroyed much of the infrastructure in Monrovia and surrounding suburbs, including the sewer systems, water supply, and electricity network. Hundreds of thousands of people fled the country or took up residence in internally displaced people (IDP) camps. Incidents of looting and harassment of citizens continued for years to come.

The Bakamo ceasefire

After losing their stranglehold on Monrovia, the NPFL became (briefly) more amenable to the idea of a peaceful settlement. Charles Taylor attended a meeting hosted by ECOWAS in Bamako Mali on 28 November 1990, where all the factions signed a ceasefire. Dr. Amos Sawyer was instated as Interim President of the Interim Government of National Unity (IGNU) and duly recognised by the INPFL and AFL. The NPFL grudgingly half-recognised his authority, only to withdraw their support of Sawyer and the IGNU in January of the following year.

By this time, ECOMOG peacekeeping forces were nine thousand strong, fifteen thousand people were dead, and over five hundred thousand Liberians had been displaced.

A fragile peace

The Bamako Ceasefire Agreement was fragile, lasting for only four months after it was signed. During that time, though fighting between the NPFL and other factions continued in the rest of the country, Monrovia, under the control of ECOMOG forces, reverted to a relatively peaceful state. It felt as though we had all paused to catch our breath. Regrettably, this did not last long.

Operating out of Monrovia, ECOMOG was tasked with coercing the warring factions to implement the measures agreed to in the ceasefire. Primarily, this involved facilitating the demobilisation of NPFL forces whose continued belligerence formed the greatest stumbling block on the road to peace.

Charles Taylor and the other heads of the NPFL, though nominally in command, had little influence over their fighters who continued, more or less autonomously, to carry out random arrests, beatings, abductions, detainments, infringements of human rights acts of violence, confiscations, and destruction of property.

The AFL, meanwhile, was supposedly under control of the IGNU and confined to its base at Camp Schieffelin on the outskirts of Monrovia. However, the AFL's diminished numbers and this restriction of movement did little to hamper its ability to act autonomously and commit heinous human rights violations right under the nose of the interim government. AFL soldiers took part in lootings, beatings, and the harassment of civilians throughout Monrovia.

The INPFL was confined to their base in Caldwell. And, like the AFL, they only technically observed the ceasefire and were, in fact, continuing to carry out similar acts of violence. Only when INPFL head Prince Johnson began sporadically executing members of his own forces on suspicion of treason did the IGNU step in. A falling out between the INPFL and the IGNU led to Johnson withdrawing from the peace process. Hence, within days of signing the agreement, the INPFL violated it by launching an attack on the AFL.

To make matters worse, the leadership of all military factions involved in the Liberian civil war had difficulties controlling their soldiers on the ground, and these soldiers committed many atrocities against civilians living in Monrovia and the surrounding areas.

Plans for disarmament

All the while, ECOWAS tried to arrange a peaceful resolution to the fighting that raged on, regardless of the Bakamo agreement. On 21 December 1990, the IGNU, NPFL, and the remnants of Doe's loyalists signed a second peace agreement in Banjul, The Gambia. But, by January 1991, Charles Taylor, whose forces now occupied ninety-five percent of the country, threw out all previously signed peace agreements.

The All-Liberia National Conference held from 15 March to 18 April 1991, just four months after the signing of the Bakamo agreement, aimed to establish mechanisms for disarmament and prepare the country for election.

At this meeting, with approval from the INPFL and AFL, the ECOWAS once again set up an IGNU, and Dr. Amos Sawyer, who had been serving as Interim President-in-Exile, was elected as President of the IGNU.

Refusing to recognise the authority of the IGNU and Sawyer's presidency, the NPFL delegation walked out of the conference after just seven days.

A dispute over the degree to which it should cooperate with the IGNU, ECOMOG, and the NPFL caused an irrevocable split in Johnson's INPFL that later led to its official disbandment in October 1992.

National Patriotic Reconstruction Assembly Government (NPRAG)

After openly rejecting the claim of the IGNU over his territories at the All-Liberian National Conference, Taylor set up a new government of his own, which he called the National Patriotic Reconstruction Assembly Government (NPRAG). He declared that the land under NPFL control would henceforth be an independent nation, known as Greater Liberia, and he would be its ruler – even insisting that everyone (including the international press and diplomats) refer to him as President Taylor, despite the conspicuous absence of any elections.

Since all the NPFL's attempts to capture Monrovia had been thwarted, Taylor set up a new legislative and administrative capital in Gbarnga Bong County, seeking to set the remote town up as the strategic centre of his vast military and administrative empire. In the following years, he and his associates would go to great lengths to instil a sense of legitimacy around Greater Liberia and NPRAG, establishing an independent banking system with its own currency, an international airfield, and a thriving, if contentious, export trade in gold, diamonds, rubber, and timber. The "country" even boasted its own radio and television network.

Along with these developments came severe limitations on the freedoms of the people of Greater Liberia. NPRAG enforced restrictions of movement, assembly, and expression in its territory, meeting all opposition with the utmost force.

The United Liberation Movement for Democracy

On 23 March 1991, a day after Taylor and his entourage had walked out of the All-Liberian National Conference, Liberian armed forces invaded Sierra Leone. Although the NPFL denied any involvement in the attack, the Liberian troops had entered Sierra Leone from NPFL-held territory, which cast aspersions on their claim, particularly given that the attack appeared to target a group of Krahn expatriates living in Sierra Leone.

The fighting began as a series of border skirmishes

between the NPFL and Sierra Leonean armed forces assisted by members of the United Liberation Movement for Democracy (ULIMO) – a pro-Doe armed coalition made up of Krahn refugees in Sierra Leone and Guinea, many of whom were former members of the AFL. Further battles erupted in Grand Gedeh County, where ULIMO forces (possibly out of Guinea) had established a formidable Krahn resistance movement.

The attack on Sierra Leone also instigated the formation of the Sierra Leonean rebel group known as the Revolutionary United Front (RUF), led by Foday Sankoh and rumoured to be backed by Taylor.

ULIMO became a formidable bush-warfare force that closely cooperated with ECOMOG, and on 11 June 1991, it issued an ultimatum to the NPFL to surrender to ECOMOG or risk being attacked. The NPFL responded by killing members of the Krahn, Mandingo, and related ethnic groups in Grand Gedeh County. This resulted in a fresh influx of refugees into Côte d'Ivoire.

ULIMO forces entered the war in Western Liberia in September 1991, and a long military engagement between ULIMO and the NPFL ensued. With fifteen thousand soldiers, ULIMO was the second biggest warring faction after the NPFL, and they soon gained control over key NPFL territories, including the diamond mining areas of Lofa and Bomi counties.

In October that same year, Taylor reluctantly signed the Yamoussoukro IV Accord, which provided for disarmament of the NPFL, the establishment of encampment factions and the handover of all territories to ECOMOG to pave the way for legitimate elections monitored by ECOMOG. However, as ULIMO did not enter the Yamoussoukro agreement and rumours of an ECOMOG-ULIMO alliance abounded, Taylor refused to disarm his troops.

Instead, driven by fear of infiltration by ULIMO forces, he clamped down upon everyone living in and entering his territories. As a result, arbitrary arrests, detentions, harassment and occasionally even execution of people suspected of being ULIMO spies were frequent occurrences, leaving civilians vulnerable once more to the whims of their military overlords.

By November 1991, reports showed that the human rights of citizens living in Greater Liberia were far less well protected than those of Liberians living in Monrovia.

ULIMO did, in fact, assist ECOMOG against the NPFL and played a key role in preventing the NPFL from capturing Monrovia.

Hopes dashed

In early 1992, there had been some hope of a diplomatic settlement. The roads leading out of Monrovia into NPFL territory opened, and Taylor permitted ECOMOG troops to inspect some areas. An Interim Election Commission, with members drawn from both NPRAG and the IGNU, was instated in January, and elections scheduled for April 1992. In March, an ad hoc Supreme Court, also comprising representatives from both factions, was sworn in. And, in the light of these promising developments, the University of Liberia reopened in April 1992.

Sadly, the elections did not take place. After being postponed twice, they were cancelled since the minimum conditions for holding elections had not been met. Obstacles to the process included continued human rights abuses, the absence of one-third of the population, as refugees in neighbouring countries, and Taylor's refusal to allow ECOMOG to deploy troops in areas under his control.

At a mini summit held in Geneva, the participants reaffirmed their commitment to the Yamoussoukro IV Accord and drew up a new timetable for ECOMOG deployment. The summit agreed to set up a buffer zone on the Sierra Leone border to separate ULIMO and NPFL forces. However, on leaving the meeting, Taylor retracted his consent, refusing to disarm or encamp his soldiers.

ECOMOG attempted to deploy its forces into Greater Liberia on 30 April 1992, but the NPFL put up strong resistance. In a gun battle in Lofa County shortly after deployment, the NPFL captured six Senegalese ECOMOG soldiers. Taylor's men reportedly slit the throats of these soldiers, prompting the withdrawal of ECOMOG troops to Monrovia.

The NPFL held hostage five hundred and eighty

ECOMOG soldiers in Greater Liberia, preventing them from joining ECOMOG's withdrawal movement. They humiliated the soldiers, beat them, stripped them of their belongings, disarmed them and detained them in NPFL camps. Taylor's troops also intercepted all communications and supplies sent to the ECOMOG soldiers from Monrovia.

In late September 1992, US President Jimmy Carter intervened, and the soldiers were allowed to return to Monrovia. The incident inflamed ECOMOG's hostility towards the NPFL, catalysing its transformation from a peacekeeping unit into a peace-enforcement unit.

The UN Security Council appealed to all factions to uphold the Yamoussoukro Accord, but to no avail. Liberia was divided into two main areas: Greater Liberia, under the control of Charles Taylor and his NPFL rebels, and Monrovia, held by ECOMOG forces.

Though the IGNU was supposed to be in control of Monrovia, they held little actual power other than that exercised by ECOMOG. Fighting, food shortages, and corruption brought the once-bustling city to its knees. If not for the efforts of the UN, Catholic Relief Services (CRS), and other foreign aid agencies, there would have been no electricity, running water or food for the five hundred thousand people still trying to eke out an existence in the city.

Taylor retained his self-instated position as president of Greater Liberia, ignoring ECOWAS's calls for disarmament, and resisting the infiltration of ECOMOG soldiers into his domain. He focussed instead on building his empire, denouncing the new "Liberty" five-dollar bill, first minted in January by the central bank in Monrovia, and prohibiting its use in Greater Liberia, where he insisted that the old bill would remain the only legal tender (except for the US dollar). Anyone caught carrying Liberty notes in his territory received hefty fines. The introduction of Liberty notes also infuriated Prince Johnson. Holed up as he was in his Caldwell base, he now had nowhere to spend the riches he had amassed in old Liberian currency during the war – except, ironically, in Taylor's territory.

Although US dollars were accepted by both sides, the official exchange rates and black-market exchange rates varied. In Monrovia, you might get between five and eight Liberian dollars for one US dollar, whereas in Greater Liberia, the exchange rate was closer to two or three to one.

Taylor also encouraged international trade, granting lucrative concessions to several foreign diamond and gold exporters, particularly from Germany and France, and allowing the Liberian-American Mining Company, one of the region's biggest iron-ore producers, to resume its exports to Europe. As a result, the taxes and export duties on timber, rubber and mining operations, which once went to the Doe government, now filled the coffers of Taylor's NPRAG.

Taylor also insisted that all international aid be shipped solely through the Port of Buchanan, which he controlled, and not through the larger port of Monrovia, which was controlled by ECOMOG.

The NPFL had swelled its ranks to about ten thousand troops, and dozens of soldiers, many of whom were boys as young as nine or ten, all carrying machine guns, manned checkpoints along all major routes.

Taylor's troops notoriously harassed and assaulted civilians and aid workers, and raped women at these checkpoints. Reports circulated of aid workers being pistol-whipped, arrested and detained (on allegations of spying) by NPFL soldiers. Relief vehicles, food, and supplies were also "confiscated".

The Liberian civilians in Greater Liberia were the ones to suffer as aid workers ultimately refused to travel into NPFL territories, saying that Taylor's use of terror and intimidation made it impossible for them to deliver aid to NPFL-controlled areas.

PART 5

1992–1993

NO END TO WAR

The Black Berets

The Black Berets were an elite security force formed by the IGNU in 1991–1992. Their mandate was to combat crime in Monrovia.

During late spring and early summer of 1992, insecurity mounted in Monrovia when a series of grenade attacks of uncertain origin left eight dead and sixty people wounded.

ECOMOG forces were powerless to stop rebels from both sides infiltrating the city, exchanging gunfire, and launching barrages of grenade attacks. Armed robberies, murders, and attacks on civilians were commonplace. Monrovian police and security officers were notorious for mishandling cases, particularly those involving sexual or gender-based violence, such as domestic abuse, child abuse, and sexual assault. And ECOMOG maintained it was beyond its remit as a peacekeeping force to perform police work. The AFL had been decimated and thus rendered ineffectual, while ULIMO forces advanced through NPFL territories towards Monrovia.

Frustration over the stalled political negotiations combined with reports of corruption, economic instability and, finally, fuel shortages led to anti-IGNU demonstrations in Monrovia, while rumour had it that Taylor's forces were preparing a fresh assault on the capital. Sawyer responded by raising an elite force known as the Black Berets.

Organised, armed, and trained in Guinea by the IGNU, this special anti-terrorist unit comprised five hundred men. They were meant to patrol the streets and help safeguard the citizens of Monrovia. However, while the intent might have been good, in reality, their presence instilled dread in the hearts of the people they were supposed to protect. Within a short time, allegations were made that they had actively participated in the violence they had been sent in to curtail. Various human rights reports suggest they took part in rapes, murders, and the intimidation of civilians while purportedly maintaining order in the city.

To this day, the legitimacy of the Black Berets remains in question, with some lauding them as instruments of peace, while others criticise them for being overly aggressive and, in some cases, criminal.

Trouble brewing

In 1992, any semblance of peace in our country was shattered. Trouble had been brewing all year long in

Greater Liberia, and it would soon wend its way into the very heart of Monrovia. Fighting between ULIMO and the NPFL continued to escalate, with ECOMOG providing arms, intelligence, and even uniforms to ULIMO forces.

Matters came to a head in August 1992, when ULIMO launched a full-scale attack from Sierra Leone into NPFL-held territory on the outskirts of Monrovia, routing the NPFL and displacing over thirty thousand people into the capital. Once again, civilians were targeted by both sides as soldiers stripped fleeing refugees of their belongings, looted villages, and executed anyone whom they suspected of siding with their opponents. Among them, a large group of civilians from the Vai and Gola ethnic groups who were massacred during the battle for control over the diamond mining centre of Tubmanburg on 24 August 1992.

By the time the dust cleared on the battle, ULIMO had captured Grand Cape Mount County, Bomi County, three quarters of Lofa County, and a part of Margibi County, as well as the Po River Bridge, just fifteen miles outside Monrovia. Eager to keep ECOMOG onside, ULIMO hastened to announce that they had no designs on taking the Caldwell base or any part of Monrovia.

Further skirmishes between the NPFL and ULIMO followed, some of which occurred close to ECOMOG positions and resulted in direct involvement of ECOMOG forces. In an incident in Brewerville on 2 October, ULIMO troops reportedly sought refuge behind ECOMOG forces.

This led to direct combat occurring between ECOMOG and the NPFL. In the end, three ECOMOG soldiers and fifty NPFL fighters died in the battle.

Taylor cracked down on alleged ULIMO informers in his territories, executing NPFL officials and civilians, and preventing people from leaving Greater Liberia. In late September, the NPFL reportedly massacred between three hundred and four hundred and fifty refugees believed to be ULIMO spies and burned down houses in Klay Bomi County.

NPFL radio broadcasts also reported harassment of local officials for failing to support Taylor's recruitment of "young men" into his army.

The Small Boys Unit

Established by Libyan leader, Muammar Gaddafi, the Small Boys Unit (SBU) initially comprised over ten thousand child soldiers between the ages of eight and ten, who were forcibly coerced into fighting for the Revolutionary United Front (RUF) during the Sierra Leone Civil War. Working with the RUF, Taylor helped to recruit child soldiers and organise them into the SBU.

Though barely any taller than the AK-47 guns that they carried, members of the SBU were especially feared because of the brutality of their attacks on soldiers and civilians alike, which frequently involved mutilation and torture. Also, many soldiers fighting against the SBU baulked at the idea of shooting children, which added to the effectiveness of the SBU forces.

In Liberia, as in Sierra Leone, Taylor's recruitment process involved the abduction of children from their villages, frequently after they had witnessed the brutal torture and murder of their family members. Traumatised and impoverished, the children were easily swayed to do whatever their captives asked in exchange for food, clothes, shelter, basic education, protection, the opportunity to show off their skills, and the promise of revenge for the deaths of their parents. They used girls as sex slaves, while the boys received militia training, which included lessons on mutilation and torture, as well as indoctrination and brainwashing under the influence of drugs (most often cocaine or LSD) and alcohol.

Taylor's SBU troops were not the only child soldiers to fight in the Liberian civil wars. According to Human Rights Watch, approximately fifteen thousand child soldiers, including both girls and boys, fought on all sides of the conflict between 1989 and 2003.

The physical and psychological trauma experienced by these children had far-reaching consequences. Many of them struggle to assimilate into society. They battle to overcome a variety of addictions and experience a spectrum of psycho-social disturbances, including nightmares, uncontrollable aggression, and strongly anti-social behaviour.

Operation Octopus

To the dismay of many ECOMOG soldiers, these unfortunate boys formed part of the twenty-five-thousand-strong NPFL force that attacked the city of Monrovia in October 1992.

Operating from his base in the Firestone Rubber Plantation, Taylor orchestrated an assault that brought the entire weight of the NPFL to bear on Monrovia, attacking the city from multiple directions like the arms of an octopus – the object being to attack from the north and east simultaneously, driving the enemy back towards the Atlantic Ocean. Taylor allegedly drugged thousands of child soldiers, told them that Monrovia had fallen, and sent them into the city to take whatever they could find and kill anyone who got in their way.

In the early hours of 15 October, at Taylor's command, Howitzer cannons and eighty-one-millimetre mortars, set up in the outer suburbs of Monrovia, launched a ceaseless barrage of artillery fire on the city. As the bomb blasts drove sleeping Monrovians from their beds, wave after wave of ruthless soldiers, many of them mere children, flooded the city. Homes and business were ransacked, grenades thrown, and people shot in the streets. So began one of the deadliest conflicts of the war.

One of the first targets was Camp Schieffelin, where the remnants of the AFL were encamped. Attacks on outlying ECOMOG posts in Monrovia followed shortly after. The modus operandi comprised initial artillery assaults, followed by brutal infantry raids.

In a move that irrefutably confirmed its transition from peacekeeper to combatant, ECOMOG responded by re-arming the AFL and forming an open alliance with ULIMO. This new alliance changed the dynamics of the war and raised concerns over ECOMOG's apparent willingness to overlook the grievous human rights violations committed by both the AFL and ULIMO. Some observers attribute the alliance to military necessity, pointing to the fact that the local AFL and ULIMO troops provided the mostly foreign ECOMOG soldiers with invaluable knowledge of the terrain, including corridors of infiltration that they used to drive the NPFL from the city.

Though the battle went on for more than a month, fighters from the ECOMOG/AFL/ULIMO alliance successfully repelled the NPFL's onslaught on Monrovia. Gardnersville, Barnersville, New Georgia, and Caldwell were especially hard hit. During the fighting, approximately two hundred thousand people were driven from their homes into the city centre. Other civilians were displaced "behind Taylor's lines" into the interior of the country.

The number of casualties and extent of the destruction escalated when ECOMOG made the mistake of leaving the AFL and ULIMO soldiers to their own devices, tasking them with patrolling the streets of Monrovia. The presence of these factions terrified citizens, who feared a resurgence of brutality and ethnic violence.

It did not take long for AFL and ULIMO troops

to resort to form, vandalising and looting the territory they were supposed to be guarding. Within a few days, ULIMO troops found their way into New Kru Town, where they harassed, assaulted, and murdered ordinary people in a terrifying onslaught. The corpses of innocent civilians soon filled the streets; horribly wounded mothers, children, and babies wrapped in blood-soaked bandages crammed into hospitals. The swamplands surrounding the capital filled up with the rotting corpses of child soldiers, many of whom clutched oversized stuffed teddy bears.

Renegade elements of the AFL (sometimes in conjunction with ULIMO) formed vigilante squads which scoured Monrovia, killing anyone they suspected of being NPFL and INPFL supporters. They particularly targeted people from Nimba County, where Taylor had a wide base of support. Although these murders were more centred on looting and pillaging, rather than the ethnic cleansing which characterised former incursions.

Sometimes, the AFL would clear out areas by telling inhabitants that the NPFL was on its way. Once an area was cleared, the soldiers ransacked the abandoned homes, stealing anything and everything, regardless of whom these items belonged to. Some even tagged the walls of homes they intended to claim as their own after the war.

Members of the NPFL also took part in raids, indiscriminate killing, and looting. They executed anyone who refused to cooperate, along with scores of IGNU officials and employees.

By the time allied soldiers appeared in the heart of the city, serious confusion arose, as some people mistook them for Taylor's men. This situation created a fresh problem for ECOMOG as it now had to take on the role of military police while simultaneously clearing the city of the very soldiers who were supposed to be its allies.

During the fighting, the INPFL base in Caldwell changed hands several times, before finally being captured by ECOMOG and ULIMO. The INPFL officially disbanded and those members who had not deserted, been killed or rejoined the NPFL (including Prince Johnson himself) surrendered to ECOMOG.

Nuns massacred in Gardnersville

The incident that, although small in scale compared to the widespread death and destruction in Monrovia, drew international attention back to the war occurred in late October. Five American nuns, and possibly four novices, were summarily executed – allegedly by NPFL soldiers, although Charles Taylor strenuously denied any involvement by his men.

The nuns were members of the Order of the Sacred Blood of Christ, based in Ruma, Illinois. It took two weeks for the bodies to be discovered. Three of them had been killed in the convent house; the two others were found in a car on a nearby road. Several more bodies were found around the convent.

Widespread terror and confusion

Contrary to Taylor's expectations that the city would fall within days, the fighting raged on for a month. By 1 November 1992, ECOMOG, assisted by the AFL, ULIMO, and five hundred troops from the Black Berets, went on the offensive and engaged in open combat with the NPFL. The presence of all these combatants left the ordinary citizens of Monrovia terrified and confused over who exactly was in control of the situation.

ECOWAS meets in Abuja

At a meeting of the ECOWAS on 7 November 1992, a communique was issued requesting a ceasefire, effective at midnight on 10 November, along with the encampment and disarmament of all warring parties, and the appointment of a special representative from the UN who would help to implement the ECOWAS peace plan. They further requested the imposition of sanctions until these conditions were met.

The ceasefire was not forthcoming, however, and on 19 November, the UN Security Council authorised an arms embargo against Liberia (ECOMOG was exempt from this embargo). Special representative Trevor Livingstone Gordon-Somers from the UN Development Program (UNDP) was appointed to evaluate the situation and report his findings to the Security Council.

The AFL makes an example

On 21 November 1992, the AFL chief of staff General Hezekiah Bowen attempted to set an example to those within its ranks who continued to engage in looting and murders of innocent civilians. The AFL court-martial board charged Private Tarwaley Mannie with the murder of a civilian whom he purportedly believed to have been a rebel. The warning intended with Mannie's public execution appears to have had little effect on the actions of AFL soldiers.

ECOMOG bombs fall on civilians

ECOMOG's shift from a peacekeeping role to an openly combatant one, brought the organisation's commitment to upholding human rights into question — not only because it allied itself with the AFL and ULIMO, both of which had committed gross human rights violations, but also because of its own actions. Critics pointed out that, besides making very little effort to curtail continued infringements committed by its allies, ECOMOG itself had conducted a series of bombing and strafing raids on NPFL-held areas, killing hundreds of civilians.

Toward the end of November 1992, having wrested control of Monrovia from the NPFL, it broadened its offensive by conducting bombing and strafing raids across Greater Liberia. Chasing Taylor and his troops from one stronghold to another, ECOMOG hit Port Buchanan, Gbarnga, Harbel, and Kakata.

Its strikes on civilian targets in these areas, such as the CRS warehouse in Buchanan on 16 November 1992, the hospital and the Firestone Plantation in Harbel, and the main commercial street in Kakata, were especially difficult to justify.

The Harbel plantation was populated by families who had been recruited by the company in its eagerness to return to business as usual. These families were incredulous when West African "peacekeeping" forces shattered the sanctuary of their compound, bombing the soccer field near Harbel where children and adults played games and relaxed. To add insult to injury, the jets returned and strafed the survivors.

Meanwhile, the NPFL continued bombarding Monrovia with artillery shells and rocket strikes well into the new year. Heavy fighting caused civilian casualties and led to the closure of Spriggs Payne Airport. And NPFL control over the White Plains water processing plant caused water shortages throughout the city.

Early 1993

The battle for control over Monrovia continued throughout December 1992 and into January 1993. The NPFL had advanced to within three miles of the city centre, before being expelled from the city by ECOMOG, ULIMO, and AFL soldiers. In late January, however, internal difficulties reopened an old rift amongst ULIMO forces, once again dividing the army into two: a mostly Krahn and non-Muslim "civilian" branch (ULIMO-J) headed by Raleigh Seekie, and an almost completely Muslim, predominantly Mandingo (Malinke) "military" branch (ULIMO-K) headed by Gen. Alhaji Kromah.

The NPFL retreat into the eastern parts of Liberia began towards the end of February 1993. ULIMO pursued the NPFL troops as they withdrew, capturing NPFL strongholds, including Roberts Airfield, Kakata, and Harbel, as well as the seaport of Buchanan, and Greater Liberia's "capital city" Gbarnga.

Refugees flow into neighbouring countries

Fleeing daily bombing raids delivered by NPFL, ULIMO, and ECOMOG, thousands of displaced Liberians once again streamed into the heart of Monrovia and across the borders into Guinea and Côte d'Ivoire. An ECOMOG general amnesty was announced on 25 February, causing significant numbers of NPFL soldiers to desert their posts, whilst others fled across to Cote d'Ivoire and the US. Charles Taylor is alleged to have gone into hiding at this time.

The Nimba Redemption Council of Liberia (NRCL)

By now, the situation in Liberia was, once again, extremely complicated. ULIMO held one third of the country, including Bomi, Cape Mount, and most of the

Lofa counties, while the Black Berets and ULIMO troops continued to occupy Monrovia.

ECOMOG claimed to be in control of the city and surrounding areas, having disarmed the ULIMO soldiers. It had also held on to control of the port of Buchanan in Grand Bassa County. ECOMOG had severely limited AFL operations within ECOMOG territory and claimed to be providing protection and security to displaced persons' camps (DPCs).

The rest of the country remained in the hands of the NPFL, except for Karpeh Dwanyen's Nimba Redemption Council of Liberia (NRCL), an anti-Taylor group based in Nimba County. Dwanyen insisted that Nimba County was not as pro-Taylor as people had been led to believe. Foremost amongst their reasons for opposing the NPFL, Dwanyen cited the execution of many leading Nimban politicians, amongst them his father David Dwanyen, at the hands of NPFL soldiers. The NRCL, reportedly boasting one thousand troops, attacked several NPFL posts and allegedly did not spare civilians during these attacks.

Aftermath

Mayhem followed the ECOMOG/AFL/ULIMO victory. AFL and ULIMO soldiers strutted around the streets of Monrovia in stolen clothing, showing off the booty they had obtained from looting the houses of innocent Monrovians. They stole cars at checkpoints and careened around town sprawled over the bonnets, hanging from car windows or piled up on trucks, guns at the ready. Things got so bad that the IGNU eventually asked ECOMOG to disarm the soldiers and get them out of the city, which they did during city-wide sweeps in late March 1993.

In the months that followed the attack on Monrovia, horrifying evidence of the extent of the carnage continued to surface, including hundreds of human skulls and decomposing corpses found in mass graves across the city. Working with members of the World Health Organization (WHO) and the Monrovia City Corporation, ECOMOG discovered the bodies of more than three thousand people, allegedly executed by Charles Taylor's NPFL forces during, or possibly after, the battle.

The Cotonou Peace Accord

By July 1993, it seemed impossible that peace would ever come to Liberia. Yet, on 25 July 1993, the IGNU, NPFL, and ULIMO gathered in Cotonou Benin and agreed to a ceasefire that was to begin on 1 August 1993. Plans were also drawn up for a provisional government to be established in September that year and for an election to take place in 1994.

Unbelievably, the deadline for the ceasefire was met, and by 17 August 1993, a five-member executive council was established that would act as the provisional government. Though peace had not been conclusively established, a feeling of guarded optimism prevailed – particularly since the NPFL (the primary dissenter to previous agreements) had been considerably weakened, having lost some of its territory and suffered economically under a series of UN and ECOWAS embargoes.

Also, ECOMOG peacekeeping forces expanded to include soldiers from countries outside of West Africa, and this time, the UN agreed to take an active role in the implementation of the peace accord.

The United Nations Observer Mission in Liberia

The UN Security Council established the UN Observer Mission in Liberia (UNOMIL), the first UN peacekeeping mission undertaken in cooperation with an existing peacekeeping operation by another organisation (ECOWAS's ECOMOG).

UNOMIL comprised a civilian component and a military component, both headquartered in Monrovia. The military wing would monitor and ensure compliance with the ceasefire, arms embargo, and the cantonment, disarmament, and demobilisation of troops. The civilian branch included political, humanitarian and electoral personnel to oversee the entire election process from end to end.

In August 1993, in cooperation with ECOMOG, UNOMIL reconnaissance missions prepared for full deployment, disarmament, and demobilisation in strategic areas of the country. To say the situation was complex was an understatement. Inherent instability in Liberia and political upheaval in neighbouring Nigeria did little to help the situation, and by mid-September, ECOMOG was redeploying troops into Monrovia in response to rumours that the NPFL planned to launch another offensive. This caused a delay in the start of disarmament. Liberian parties disagreed on the distribution of ministerial portfolios, as well as dates for the seating of the transitional government and for the beginning of encampment, disarmament, and demobilisation of combatants.

PART 6

1993–1995

MONROVIA

Return to Monrovia

All the time I lived with Ornekel in Gbarnga, my thoughts kept drifting back to my family. I had lost touch with them when the war broke out, and we were all forced to flee the city. Every day, I mourned their loss. I feared for their safety, worried about their welfare. *Where were they now? Had they found shelter? Did they have enough to eat? Were they safe? Had the fighters got to them?* I could not bring myself to think about what might have happened to them if they had fallen prey to these evil men. Instead, I prayed fervently to God that He would keep them safe from harm. The burden of longing to find them, and yet, being unable to go back to Monrovia, weighed heavily upon me throughout my time in Gbarnga.

One day, in November 1993, we received news that Monrovia, being under IGNU and ECOMOG control, was the safest place in Liberia. Despite it having been the scene of a brutal attack by **NPFL** forces in recent months, the fighting had moved away from the city into the interior of the country, and, aside from severe overcrowding, and occasional incidents of abuse at the hands of renegades (and, in some cases, the Monrovian police), life in Monrovia was relatively peaceful. Roads into and out of the city had opened up, and it was safe to travel once more.

This news delighted me. The prospect of returning to Monrovia and possibly being reunited with my family excited me. So, I told Ornekel, "It's time for me to go back to Monrovia. I have to find my family." She understood my situation completely and agreed that I should take advantage of the relative peace and go home. We put the idea to her father, and he kindly offered to take me there in his commercial vehicle.

A city in ruins

My desperation to find my family and my concern for their safety intensified as soon as I reached the city. So, I went directly to New Kru Town on Bushrod Island, where my sister Diana had lived before the war. The devastation I saw along the way shocked me to the core. Almost all the buildings had been damaged, and the infrastructure destroyed. It broke my heart to see this once grand city reduced to rubble, its people destitute, homeless, and starving.

THOUGH YOU SLAY ME

Reunion

Although the city was relatively peaceful, travelling through Monrovia was far from safe. Aside from the harassment, rapes, and beatings that were a common occurrence at the various checkpoints, it was also easy to become caught in the crossfire of sporadic bombing and fighting that continued to erupt throughout the city. So, I picked my way carefully through the desolate streets.

From time to time, I heard shooting and grenades exploding, and I ran for cover, my heart beating hard against my ribs. But most times, the fighting was some distance away from me, and so I hurried on. Avoiding known hot spots, dodging both the ECOMOG forces and the dreaded Black Berets as best I could, I ran the gauntlet until, eventually, I entered New Kru Town.

Those hours I spent on the streets of Monrovia were among the most fearful of my life, but it was all worth it in the end. As soon as I got into New Kru Town, I began asking around after my sister and her family. It did not take long before I found someone who told me that, yes, she was still living in the same house. They showed me the safest way to get there, and with tears blurring my vision, I ran as fast as I could.

I stopped on the doorstep of my sister's house, trying to catch my breath. I was just about to knock when the door swung open to reveal a boy of about twelve or thirteen. For a moment, I stood frozen beneath the gaze of his big brown eyes, then a dam of emotion broke within me. I reached out and took him into my arms. Chris let me hug him for a lot longer than a teenager would probably feel comfortable with these days, and I will be forever grateful for that. He gently extricated himself from my grasp and ushered me inside.

My sister ran over to us and embraced me in a bear hug. We cried and hugged each other several times. Then we all started talking at once.

I spent a few days with them. At the time, Chris did not know I was his mother. He still called me "Aunty". But that did nothing to dampen my spirits. I was overjoyed to see my boy and impressed by how well-mannered, caring and handsome he was. My sister and her husband had brought him up as their own child, and they had taken good care of him. They had kept him safe throughout the war and ensured that he went to school and got a solid education. I was so proud to see that he had grown into a fine young man.

Once we had gotten over the initial excitement of being reunited, I asked my sister whether she had news of the rest of our family. She told me that Caroline and my cousins had found safe passage to the US. Uncle Bennie had spent time there before I was born, and his US citizenship made them eligible for evacuation by the American Red Cross.

"What about Uncle Bennie?" I asked anxiously. "Where's he?"

My heart plummeted when I saw the grief on my sister's face.

"I'm so sorry, my dear, but Uncle Bennie is dead. The rebels killed him."

I shook my head in disbelief. "No, there must be some mistake." *Not Uncle Bennie. Surely not. He was the best of us. How could these men take him from us?*

I looked from my sister to Chris and back again. Wordlessly pleading with them to tell me it was just a misunderstanding. A case of mistaken identity. These things happen. But they both just shook their heads. I saw tears rolling down their cheeks and felt the same hot tracks down my own. "It can't be," I whispered. Then I gave in to my grief and sobbed into my hands.

With tears flowing freely, my sister came over and comforted me as I wept – for Uncle Bennie, for all the innocent people murdered at the checkpoints, for the old people who had fallen along the road to Gbarnga, for the infants left to die alone, for the mothers and for all the innocent lives stolen by the war. I continued to weep for Uncle Bennie over the following days and nights, and his death still pains me to this day.

I spent a few weeks with Chris and my sister's family in New Kru Town. During that time, I was fortunate enough also to reconnect with other members of my extended family. Although times were hard, we were happy for a while.

When things took a turn for the worst in New Kru Town, my sister's family moved to Tubman Boulevard in Congo Town, and I went with them.

Naomi

I met Naomi by chance one fateful day while I was trying to hail a taxi into town. When the taxi pulled up, I hurried towards it and almost bumped into a woman of about my age headed for the same vehicle.

"Oh! I'm sorry," she said. "I didn't see you there."

"That's okay," I replied, trying to hide my annoyance. I had got one hand on the door handle and was about to yank it open and hop in, when I felt a sudden flood of sympathy for the woman. An idea struck.

"Where are you headed?" I asked her. It turned out we intended to follow more or less the same route, so we shared the cab.

While we sat side by side in the car, she introduced herself as Naomi. I told her my name, and we got to talking. After a while, I mentioned things were quite cramped where I was living with my sister and her family, and that I had been looking for somewhere nearby to rent that would not be too dear. Naomi brightened immediately. "I'm actually looking for a roommate," she said. "You could come stay with me if you like?"

I went over to her place the following day and agreed to move in with her. Naomi and I hit it off straight away, and we quickly became the best of friends, doing everything together. We went all around Monrovia, looking for food and money, both of which were in short supply. Once more, I had to rely on my looks to stop myself from starving.

ECOMOG: Friend or foe?

Regardless of the signing of the ceasefire agreement, the NPFL remained in control of almost the entire country, except for Monrovia, which was controlled by ECOMOG.

Sentiment towards ECOMOG was divided. Many Monrovians at the time said, "Thank God for ECOMOG." And the commonly held conception was that ECOMOG had achieved a measure of success between August and November 1990 by establishing a semblance of order and peace in the beleaguered city of Monrovia, allowing international humanitarian groups to return to Liberia. It had also confined the AFL and INPFL to their barracks, and it had overseen the installation of the IGNU and the appointment of Amos Sawyer. In 1993, it had coerced all parties into signing a ceasefire – however tenuous.

Foreign observers agreed that some of ECOMOG's most important accomplishments were a significant reduction in the killing of Krahn and Mandingo people in Monrovia and the successful containment of the conflict, at least for a short period, which prevented the situation from degenerating into genocidal proportions of the all-out slaughter seen in Somalia and Rwanda.

People on the street, however, saw a different side of ECOMOG. Its commanders and soldiers were notoriously underpaid and frequently engaged in looting, sending the stolen goods back to their own countries. These actions led to the popular catchphrase, "ECOMOG stands for 'Every Car Or Moving Object Gone.'"

ECOMOG commanders also allegedly sold arms and ammunition to all factions, including the NPFL, which, if true, flew in the face of the disarmament that was supposed to be its aim.

Life in Monrovia under ECOMOG

Life in Monrovia under ECOMOG was far from pleasant. The supposed "peacekeeping" forces imposed strict rules of conduct and curfews on the citizens of Monrovia, and dealt swiftly and violently with anyone who, however accidentally, did not comply with their demands.

To make things worse, there was no consistency. ECOMOG changed the curfew times without warning. One day, we would be confined to our homes from six in the morning to six in the evening; the next, our curfew would be from ten in the morning until six in the evening. Contravening curfew or any of the other restrictions ECOMOG placed on us had dire consequences. Although Naomi and I did our best to adjust to the constraints of living under ECOMOG, those were terrifying times.

Same as in Gbarnga, the biggest challenge was finding food. Whenever anyone (man or woman) went out to look for food, they could easily be snatched up, beaten, raped and murdered by soldiers from various factions (some of whom remained in Monrovia).

Naomi and I shared a flat with several other women, and we were all forced to sell our bodies or die of starvation. Money was worthless; sex was the only currency the soldiers accepted.

As long as there was a steady supply of children and very young girls to satisfy their evil desires, they seldom wanted "older" women, such as Naomi and me. But we had to eat, so out on the street we went. Often, we would come home late, exhausted and starving, having had no "luck".

When we got any food at all, it was always the same – rice wrapped in sweet potato leaves. Some people got meat or fish to make curry, but we never did. Instead, we went home each night and sobbed into our pillows. Hunger gnawed at me, and my stomach ached constantly. I lay awake at night, doubled over in pain, listening to my belly growling, overwhelmed by the fear that I would not be able to find food for the next day.

Part of the problem was how far we had to walk to find food – it could be two to three miles or more before you would find a pub or restaurant where you could beg for food. So, more often than not, we would still be out and about long after curfew, and we got arrested by ECOMOG troops many times.

When they caught us, they took away our shoes

(so we could not run away), seized anything of value that we had on us (very little by this time), and forced us to get into their vehicles. They took us to the ECOMOG base in Caldwell and kept us there overnight.

    The soldiers administered varying degrees of punishment and humiliation, depending on our alleged infringements. For instance, they forced us to roll around in a pit filled with dirty water until we were covered in mud and filth. They made us serve them, doing all sorts of menial jobs, such as carrying water for their baths. If we did not perform these tasks to their satisfaction, they insulted us, spat on us and thrashed us. We were bitterly mistreated. They held us captive, and when they finally allowed us to leave; we had to make our own way home on foot – dirty and ashamed of the things they had forced us to do.

    One particularly desperate night, when we had not eaten for many days, Naomi and I stayed out past curfew, hoping against hope that tonight we would not go to bed hungry. We were half-hidden in the entrance to a building, discussing whether to quit or continue searching when a particularly vicious ECOMOG patrol spotted us. The men on the back of the truck whooped, hollered and wolf-whistled at us, grabbing their crotches and gyrating their hips. The driver pulled the vehicle up to the curb, and a gang of them hopped out, guns at the ready, blocking our escape.

    "What have we here?" one soldier sneered. A dense

rash of purple pockmarks covered his cheeks and forehead, and his narrow black eyes gave him the look of a snake about to strike. I instinctively shrank away from him.

"Two lovely Liberian ladies. And they're out past curfew. Practically begging for it," said an equally terrifying soldier. He made the same lewd gesture the men in the truck had made, and they all laughed uproariously.

Their use of English made me realise they were Nigerians. Though the ECOMOG soldiers came from various countries, it seemed to me that the Nigerians were always the worst. I swallowed hard and croaked out a response, "Good evening, sirs. We are sorry. We got lost. We're on our way home now." I tried desperately to talk our way out of this terrible situation, knowing full well that it was useless. Unlike at the checkpoints where my knowledge of Grebo had saved me so many times, my ability to speak English did little to ingratiate me to the Nigerians.

Naomi and I clutched each other. I could feel her shaking in my arms. My knees were knocking together in terror. Both of us instinctively knew this time things would be much worse than at any other time we had been arrested.

A serious-looking soldier wearing a brown beret, who appeared to be their leader, got out of the passenger seat and swaggered over, beating his palm with an ebony baton. "What's going on here?" he demanded. "Why are you fools taking so long?"

"This one," the one with the scarred face, jabbing a

finger in my direction, "thinks she can say sorry, and we'll let them go." The others chuckled.

The leader swore. "Since when do we hold conversations with criminals? Get them into the back of the truck with the others and stop wasting time." His men hastened to obey, and they threw us into the back of the open truck. A group of terrified women who had been rounded up earlier that evening shuffled up to make room for us.

The soldiers jumped up after us, keeping their guns at the ready, should any of us try anything. We knew better. Once the leader was back in the truck, they started taunting us again.

"Look at that one," said Scarface, pointing at a young girl on the far side of the truck bed. "She's got such lovely big breasts. I'm going to have some fun with her later."

"Oh yes," the others agreed in unison.

"That little one is all mine," said his mate, waving the barrel of his gun toward a tiny girl in a tattered dress. The soldier had a large mole over his left eye that caused the eyelid to droop a little, as though he was permanently giving a salacious wink. It made me shudder to look at him. The girl could not have been more than twelve years old.

The soldiers leered at her and made suggestive remarks about how they intended to rape her later. This aggravated the guy with the mole, who turned on his fellows, so that the rifle he held swung wildly. "You lot better not get any ideas," he snapped. "I'm telling you right now, she's all mine." After that outburst, they all stopped laughing and shut up for a few seconds. But it did not take long for the cruel banter to start up again. They went through each one of us, calling us terrible names, pointing out our assets, criticising our flaws, and talking at length about the hideous acts they would perform with us. This continued as we drove on into the night.

The women around me cried in fear and anguish, but the callous soldiers carried on as if we were nothing but mannequins, devoid of thoughts and feelings. As far as they were concerned, we were simply playthings to use and abuse as they saw fit. I could not believe that we were treated this way by the very troops that were supposed to be protecting us.

When the truck finally pulled up at the ECOMOG camp in Caldwell, we were all sore and exhausted. We had been jostled and jolted against the metal base and sides of the truck and tormented by the guards the entire time. Now that we had finally reached our destination, the soldiers pointed their rifles at us. "Get up, you lazy good-for-nothings," said Scarface, poking the woman nearest him in the ribs with his rifle. His friends followed suit. We all obeyed and hastily disembarked from the vehicle.

They immediately marched us into a nearby prison cell. There was nothing in it except an already half-filled bucket that was supposed to serve as a toilet. The stench was overwhelming. Gagging, we meekly entered the stinking cell. We had all seen firsthand what happened to anyone who dared disobey the soldiers, and we had no desire to bring that fate onto ourselves.

When the cell door clanged shut, relief washed over us. We made ourselves as comfortable as possible on the cold concrete floor. Some women tried to sleep, but for all except the oldest amongst us, sleep simply would not come. We knew this was only a temporary reprieve. The soldiers would be back soon enough.

They came for the twelve-year-old girl first. She cried, writhed and lashed out at her captors like a cat in a sack, but they swatted away her attacks as though she were nothing more than a pesky fly. Two of them grabbed her arms and lifted her up between them. The girl went limp, not bothering to lift her feet at all. Her rage dissolved into sobs as the soldiers dragged her out of the cell towards their barracks. We never saw her again. Later, I glimpsed her tattered yellow dress sticking out of a pile of rubbish behind the soldiers' latrine building, and it broke my heart.

They took the rest of us, one by one, throughout the night. My turn came at six the next morning. Though I had spent the night in fearful anticipation of the moment that they would choose me, words cannot adequately describe the terror I felt when they pointed their rifles at me and demanded that I come with them. My heart dropped into my belly and then bounced back up again, making me feel ill. I felt pins and needles all over my skin, and my stomach felt watery and loose, as though my bowels would betray me at any moment. My palms were wet, and my mouth was dry as I rose, trembling, to my feet.

"Get moving, you stupid cow. We haven't got all day." The soldier with the large mole pressed his gun into my back, making me stumble forward. Desperately, I prayed to God to give me the strength to endure whatever would come next.

They marched me over to the familiar filthy pond, which we all knew contained not only mud and water but also faeces and urine. "Here we go again," I thought as they lined me up on the edge of the pond. But this time, instead of forcing me into the pond at gunpoint, one soldier swung his leg and kicked me squarely in the back. His army boot struck me so hard that I flew face-first into the filthy water. The soldiers on the bank all cheered. "Now wallow in it like the sow that you are," they shouted. I hesitated. I heard the metallic clatter of rifles being pointed at me. So, I did as they told me, rubbing the filth all over my hair, my clothes, my bare skin and finally, though it made me wretch, across my face.

"Okay, now get out of there, sow." I obeyed, but as soon as I got out and stood there dripping and shivering in the morning breeze, another would come and kick me back down into the muck. This game of theirs carried on for what felt like ages, until my body went numb, my eyes stung from mud and dirty water dripping into them, and my skin shrivelled up from the constant moisture. I was beyond exhausted. My knees and palms were grazed and bleeding from the many times I had fallen on them after the soldiers pushed or kicked me to the ground.

Finally, they led me back to the prison cell. I was soaked to the skin and smelled as bad as the latrine bucket. The other older women had suffered the same treatment, and we huddled together, far too frightened and exhausted to care about the smell. Without exchanging a word, we took comfort from one another. But our tormentors had not finished with us yet.

Within a few minutes, they were back. This time, they carried wooden fighting sticks. We cowered closer together, thinking that they would lay into us with those sticks, but this only made them guffaw. "Stop that, you dumb cows," said mole guy. "Get up, come over here and take a stick." We all stood up and stared at him. Beside the man, a young soldier stood holding an armful of sticks. We looked at him and then back to the guy with the mole, uncertain whether we had heard correctly. Did he honestly mean to give us each a weapon?

The soldier with the mole let out a string of expletives. Then he pointed his rifle at us, told us to stop being such slow and stupid animals, and demanded that we each take a stick. We hurried over and got our sticks.

"Now," said the mole, "We want to see you beating each other." Once again, we hesitated. The soldier grabbed the nearest woman and put his rifle barrel right up against her temple. "Do it," he ordered, "or I'll put a bullet in her brain, and I'll keep going until there's a bullet in every one of your heads. Am I making myself clear?"

So, with tears in our eyes, we began to beat each other. If we showed any signs of dealing out mild blows or slacking off, the soldier would grab one of us and threaten to blow her brains out in front of us. Some women cried out in agony, others begged for mercy and cowered in shame. But my terror had turned to rage, and I was determined not to give the soldiers the satisfaction of seeing me broken and weeping. Instead, I kept praying, and God gave me the strength to bite my lip and keep quiet.

After what seemed like an eternity, our captors grew bored and told us we could stop. We threw down the weapons and immediately ran over to comfort the women brutalised by the beatings. There was blood and gore all over the cell, and most of us could barely stand up.

"You filthy whores can go now," Scarface told us, opening the cell door and standing aside to let us hobble past. "I hope you have all learned your lesson to obey our curfews and laws. They are there for your protection, after all." He delivered this last line with a sarcastic sneer.

The soldiers herded us out of the compound and onto the road at rifle-point. Once we had passed out of the gates, they told us to clear off. We made our slow way home. The journey by truck had taken twenty-five minutes. On foot, as terrified, exhausted and injured as we were, it would take many hours. But we had no choice. So, supporting each other amidst the throng of filthy, bedraggled, scared and shaken women, we picked our way painfully over rough roads in thin shoes and tattered clothing until we reached our homes. Many times, on that journey, I was so overcome by the weight of the trauma we had endured that I felt like sinking to my knees and crawling in the dust. But I did not want our tormentors to think that they had won, so I stayed on my feet, gritted my teeth and pressed on.

The realisation that the ECOMOG soldiers were almost as bad as the rebels when it came to exploiting our people – especially our women – was just another in a long series of bitter disappointments that Liberians had been facing since Samuel Doe took power in 1989. All these insults, abuses, and violations at the hands of so-called "peacekeeping" troops were just pieces of the heartbreaking puzzle.

I often wonder whether perhaps we were too trusting. I have travelled a lot in my life, and in my travels, I have noticed that what makes Liberians different from other people is that we are very trusting. Mostly that is a wonderful thing, but during the war, I felt we trusted too much. There were many evil men out there, and I sometimes feel that we should have been more aware that not everyone would deliver what we wanted. Perhaps that would have made the war easier to bear.

THOUGH YOU SLAY ME

Marco Carto

One evening, after a particularly hard day scouring the streets for food, Naomi said, "Let's go out."

"I've been out all day," I complained. "All I want to do is lie down for a bit."

"Come on," she insisted. "There's no use moping around here all evening. Besides, I just heard that a fresh lot of foreigners have come to town. Let's go out and meet some. You never know…"

Reluctantly, I agreed to go, though all I really felt like doing was curling up and going to sleep. Little did I know it then, but that decision changed the course of my life.

Naomi and I were standing by the side of the road, trying to hail a taxi, when a car pulled up in front of us. I could tell immediately that it wasn't a taxi, but a private car. Inside sat three White gentlemen. One of them rolled down his window and leaned out. He flashed us a toothy smile as he said in heavily accented English, "Well, aren't you two ladies lovely?" We smiled back at him and tilted our heads in a coquettish way that White men seemed to find fetching. The man's smile broadened. "Do you want to take a ride with us, then?" He asked with an ever-so-slight American twang so that it sounded more like "Do ya wanna". The man in the backseat opened the door, certain that we would say yes. Naomi, always more confident and outgoing than me, smiled back, said, "Sure." With that, she jumped into the car. I hesitated for just a few moments until the hunger pains in my stomach propelled me to follow her into the dark interior of their car.

I sat down on the cool black leather of the backseat, swung my legs in and pulled the door closed after me. The man in the backseat asked Naomi to switch places with him. He wanted to be in the middle. She hopped up onto his lap and slid down onto the far side of the seat. The man turned to me. He stuck out his hand and said, "Hi, I'm Marco Carto, but you can just call me Marco. Pleased to meet you." I gingerly took the proffered hand and gave it a brief shake before withdrawing my hand back into my lap.

"I'm Rita."

Not to be outdone, Naomi also stuck her hand out and introduced herself. Marco shook her hand politely, but it didn't take too long before his gaze swung back to me. He had lovely dark brown eyes, caramel skin, and thick black hair that swept across his forehead in a smooth curve. From the way his hair shone, even in the dim light within the car, you could tell that he oiled it. He was clean-shaven with just a hint of dark stubble, which showed that he would be quite capable of growing a thick, lustrous beard and matching moustache. He smelled divine – like clean linen and sandalwood. Though he wore little in the way of jewellery, I could not help but notice his fine clothes, well-manicured hands and high-quality shoes. He clearly liked me, and I remember thinking that if I played this right, I might go to bed with a full belly that night, if nothing else.

The two other men in the car chatted away as we

sped through the streets towards the more affluent part of town. They introduced themselves as David and Lorenzo and told Naomi and me they were bankers from Italy. Naomi looked across at me and winked when they said this. We, that is Naomi and I, had a duty to provide food and shelter for our families, and it was very fortunate for both of us to have met these men. They were well-mannered and had plenty of money, which they did not mind spending on us in exchange for the pleasure of our company.

Marco and I developed a romantic relationship of sorts, though it was based on pragmatism rather than love. I was young, beautiful, and poor. He was older, wealthy, and attracted to me. I can honestly say I did not love him. We simply enjoyed each other's company and kept things casual. Things are different now. I have a far deeper view of relationships and what they entail – one that allows space for love. But in those days, we didn't have such luxuries.

When I was not out with Marco, I spent a lot of time trying to find my sister and Christopher, who had been displaced during the battle for Monrovia. I was desperate not to lose touch with them and jeopardise the tenuous bond that had just started to form between Chris and me two years earlier.

I gave thanks to God for Marco. He was very generous and helped me to locate my family. He also gave me the means to help my sister and other relatives.

The hard times were far from over, but Marco made that period of my life much more bearable than it might have been. Fun-loving Marco took me to all sorts of places. Our dates included day trips to the beach, and evenings spent dancing the night away at various nightclubs around the city. We also attended house parties and dinners together. Wherever we went, we always had a lot of fun. With Marco by my side, I made the best of life during the period of relative calm between 1993 and 1995.

When rumours of renewed fighting began to circulate in 1995, and the cycles of violence and hunger from the previous years looked set to return, Marco told me of his decision to leave the country and return to Italy.

"I'm sorry, Rita, but I have to go. It's unsafe for me here." I was not bitter. I knew what lay ahead, and I didn't blame him for wanting to leave. Nor did I expect him to take me with him. Though we had casually discussed the possibility of marriage in the past, we never tied the knot. We simply did not feel that way about each other. Even if he had made the offer, I would have dreaded the thought of leaving my country to live in a foreign land with this man. So, I made my peace with it – he had to leave, and though I was afraid of how I would survive without his financial assistance, I had to stay.

In the end, Marco gave me his car and a substantial amount of money before he left, for which I was very grateful.

News of my grandparents

I learned of my grandparents' deaths during a visit to my sister in 1995. They had stayed in our home village throughout their entire lives, and all the chaos and dangers of the war made it impossible for any of us to visit them. Fortunately, they had been spared the violent deaths suffered by so many during those times. My grandmother was ninety when she died in her sleep, and my grandfather, having contracted an unknown illness, followed shortly after her. He reached the ripe old age of one hundred and ten. So, we consoled ourselves that both these lovely people had lived long, full lives.

Everyone said that my grandfather acted with grace and dignity right up to the end of his life. He even made friends with the rebels who occupied their village – insisting when they stormed the village that they were not coming to kill him. Somehow, he got them to listen. That was his way. It was a relief in some ways that they had died of old age and natural causes, but my heart still aches that we could not be there for them and take care of them in their old age. Most especially, I regret not having the opportunity to say goodbye. The memory of these two wonderful people will always remain with me, and I trust that, God-willing, we will be reunited one day.

PART 7

1994–1996

THE STRUGGLE FOR PEACE

A humanitarian crisis

While I was trying to live a relatively "normal" life and making the best of the brief respite from the war, the higher-ups were working to disarm the warring parties and bring about peace. This was no simple task.

In January 1994, UNOMIL deployed military observers throughout Liberia and battalions of fresh ECOMOG soldiers arrived within the month. Ten encampment sites were identified, and the parties agreed to simultaneous disarmament over a two-to-three-month period.

By April, UNOMIL had military observers stationed in twenty-seven of the thirty-nine projected sites with four regional headquarters at Monrovia (central region), Tubmanburg (western region), Gbarnga (northern region) and Tapeta (eastern region). The military observers patrolled border crossings and other entry points, observed and verified disarmament and demobilisation and investigated ceasefire violations.

ECOMOG peacekeepers were deployed in the western and northern regions. However, instability in Upper Lofa prevented the deployment of both UNOMIL and ECOMOG troops to the far northern region. The Liberian Peace Council (LPC), which had emerged in July 1993, similarly prevented peacekeeping missions from entering the south-east. UNOMIL and ECOMOG engaged in consultations with ULIMO, the NPFL, and LPC in order to decide on further deployment in the western and south-eastern regions.

In the first month of disarmament, over two thousand of the approximately sixty thousand combatants from all parties were disarmed and demobilised. However, things slowed down due to ongoing hostilities and mistrust between the various parties. By the end of the third month, the total came to just under three thousand two hundred.

On 20 April 1994, the Council of State of the Liberian Transitional Government was fully installed, and Ministers for Justice, Defence, and Finance appointed. At the same time, fresh fighting broke out.

An age-old rift between the two ULIMO branches resulted in a resurgence of violence in the western region, whilst the NPFL and LPC came to blows in the east. The transitional government, ECOMOG, and UNOMIL worked together to bring about a ceasefire between the warring ULIMO factions on 6 May; only to see it collapse again before the end of the month. All attempts to quell hostilities between the NPFL and the LPC failed.

As June approached, the country faced an unprecedented humanitarian crisis, with more than a million people receiving humanitarian aid, and approximately four thousand more without access to aid because of factional fighting. In the six months since the start of the year, an additional one hundred and fifty thousand people had been displaced, and a mere seventy percent of the food requirement had been distributed.

The situation dragged on with little improvement, despite the signing of a supplementary peace agreement in September 1994. The Akosombo Agreement was signed by the NPFL, both wings of ULIMO and the AFL, but not the LPC and the Lofa Defence Force (LDF) – a second faction to emerge after Cotonou. In it, the parties committed to an immediate ceasefire and to prepare for an election that would be held in 1995.

Shortly after signing, the Akosombo Agreement became the object of great controversy, and as a result, it was never implemented. Throughout September and October 1994, the military situation remained confused, with factions switching allegiance as and when it suited their purposes. The fighting consisted mainly of smaller skirmishes, across the country, in which civilians were massacred, villages decimated, and law and order completely wiped out.

Liberia in a desperate state

Instability in the interior made the movement of relief supplies impossible, leaving thousands without aid and bringing international humanitarian aid operations to a standstill.

Unarmed UN military observers were harassed, assaulted and even used as pawns, as was the case when forty-three UNOMIL observers and six non-government organisation (NGO) personnel were detained at nine NPFL sites across the northern and eastern regions. NPFL members confiscated vehicles, communications equipment, and anything else of value. It took several days of round-the-clock talks with faction representatives, NPFL interlocutors, neighbouring countries, and ECOMOG for UNOMIL to secure the release of thirty-three of them.

The warring factions' refusal to honour the ceasefire and ECOMOG's evident inability to provide security for UNOMIL observers made it impossible for UNOMIL to perform its duties, and as a result, all UNOMIL sites were evacuated, except for those in the Monrovia area. By mid-October, only ninety of the original three hundred and sixty-eight military personnel remained in Liberia. A similar reduction in UNOMIL civilian staff accompanied the military withdrawal.

Seeking a political strategy to stop the country from sliding deeper into chaos, the Secretary-General dispatched a high-level mission to the ECOWAS countries to find a solution that would assist Liberia in bringing about a cessation of hostilities. He also recommended that the mandate of UNOMIL be extended for two months.

In November 1994, reports estimated that the crisis had affected over seven hundred thousand innocent civilians in rural Liberia, and one-point-two million residents and displaced persons in Monrovia and surrounds. With continued fighting severely restricting relief activities and not even the minimum of security conditions met, the UN could do little to ease the suffering of the Liberian people.

Several more attempts were made to bring about a ceasefire and deliver crucial humanitarian aid throughout the first half of 1995, but these had very little effect. Fighting continued throughout eighty percent of the country, and ECOMOG had been deployed in less than fifteen percent. UNOMIL's mandate was continuously extended until, on 30 June 1995, the Security Council announced a final extension that would end on 15 September 1995 and not be renewed unless substantial progress had been made towards peace.

The Abuja Agreement

Things started looking hopeful in August 1995, when, in accordance with the Abuja Agreement, a comprehensive ceasefire was established by midnight on 26 August, and a new six-member Council was installed on 1 September. Ceasefire Violations and Disarmament Committees were set up, and the humanitarian situation in several regions also improved with the opening of critical roads from Kakata to Gbarnga and Bong Mines.

As a result of these improvements, UNOMIL received a new mandate that included monitoring compliance with the ceasefire, disarmament, and demobilisation, as well as investigating and reporting on human rights violations, assisting local human rights groups, conducting intensive patrols, and creating an atmosphere conducive to free and fair elections.

Sadly, it did not take long for fresh fighting to erupt as, in December 1995, ECOMOG forces tried to wrest control of the Tubmanburg diamond mines from Roosevelt Johnson's ULIMO-J branch. Further clashes occurred between the various cabinet ministers' factions in Monrovia. Additionally, Council calls for Johnson's arrest in March and April ignited widespread fighting across the city. This fighting continued, and 1996 saw some of the war's deadliest battles.

A turn for the worse

Full-blown chaos erupted in the early hours of 6 April 1996, and once again, Monrovia transformed from a relatively peaceful place into a war zone.

It all happened very quickly, taking many of us off-guard, and many innocent civilians found themselves in the middle of the fighting.

NPFL, ULIMO-J, and other Krahn fighters who had covertly infiltrated the city drew on caches of smuggled arms and ammunition, and the violence escalated rapidly. The sound of gunfire echoed through the streets and rocket-propelled grenades whined overhead, exploding all across the city. Two aircraft hit by rocket fire exploded into flames at the airport. Not even the UN observer compound was spared, with a mortar round exploding inside its walls.

Once again, drunk and marijuana-high fighters brandishing weapons roamed the streets of Monrovia, looting businesses, breaking into homes and assaulting civilians. Over three hundred vehicles were stolen by armed men who raced around the city streets in them, harassing citizens. A group of NPFL fighters bearing arms brazenly stalked around the US embassy compound, ostensibly searching for ULIMO soldiers. Fighting also broke out around the airport, at Barclay Training Centre, and in the Mamba Point area. The violence escalated with the influx of additional NPFL and ULIMO-K troops from the countryside. Combatants pillaged aid organisational buildings and warehouses. Chaos and terror reigned throughout Monrovia with peacekeeping forces abandoning their posts and retreating into their bases, doing nothing to intervene during the pillaging and fighting, and in many cases, actively participating in the looting. Many Nigerian soldiers, who had not been paid in four months, sold ammunition or handed over arms to the Krahn soldiers. Firsthand accounts were also given of Guinean peacekeeping troops joining in the looting and selling weapons to fighters. Though ECOMOG tanks patrolled the streets in parts of the city, they were unable to restore order.

Heavy fighting between the NPFL, ULIMO-J, and the Krahn militia occurred in parts of Monrovia. Smoke from grenade explosions and fires set by looters choked the city.

The Krahn faction and Johnson's ULIMO-J troops held peacekeepers hostage against NPFL attacks in the Barclay Training Centre, which received barrages of machine-gun fire and rocket-propelled grenades. Gangs of armed youths swaggered around the central business district and Bushrod Island, looting businesses and setting them on fire.

Faced with all this violence, the US embassy requested military support from US forces to assist with the evacuation of US and foreign citizens. By Easter Sunday 7 April, more than four hundred US and foreign citizens and humanitarian aid workers awaited evacuation. The US embassy also provided sanctuary to fifteen thousand displaced Liberians at its Graystone compound.

A joint task force was established, headed by U.S. Army Brigadier General Michael A. Canavan, the commanding general of European Special Operations Command. Dubbed "Operation Assured Response" the mission was tasked with protection of US citizens and designated third- and host-country nationals in Monrovia, and their safe evacuation from the country. After nine days of bitter fighting, US forces had rescued over two thousand two hundred non-combatants hailing from seventy-three countries.

The US Marines

Unlike the ECOMOG fighters, the US marines treated us well. They saw us as people rather than objects for their own gratification. They would sit and talk to us when they saw us out and about, and occasionally, they would even buy us beer.

By this point, most of us were savvy enough to know we needed to get out of the country, and that the Westerners moonlighting on our soil might be our best ticket. Yet none of them ever offered to take us away.

Sierra Leone

Eventually, I realised I couldn't continue living as I was, wishing for someone to swoop in and rescue me. I decided to take matters into my own hands. Using the money Marco had given me, I arranged to travel to Sierra Leone. Once there, I planned to buy things to sell back in Liberia. With a little luck, the profits from this venture might give us some money to live on for a while.

So, after bidding a tearful farewell to my friends and family, I boarded a boat and off I went – hoping against hope that my plan would work, and I could make enough money to keep myself and my family safe and alive.

The boat was crowded with people from Sierra Leone and numerous Liberians who, like me, were trying to escape the harsh conditions caused by the long years of war in our country. It took three weeks to get to Sierra Leone, so we had to find ways to pass the time. Some people played cards, while others played board games, such as Choko, Yote, or Liberian Queah. No one really wanted to discuss the things that had happened to us during the war. So, we spent our days and nights sharing stories about our families and our lives before the war and listening to the Sierra Leonean people talk about life in their country.

When we arrived at the port of Freetown, we all had to wait in a long queue while the immigration officers checked our papers. By the time this was all done, I was exhausted. So, I picked up my bags and made my way out into the bustling, dusty streets. I took a taxi to a guesthouse in the city where I stayed for a month. The following day, I began looking for items that I could take back to Liberia and sell for a small profit.

Walking the streets of Freetown, I was amazed by how much the customs and traditions of the Sierra Leonean people resembled those of my own people. Even their manner of dress reminded me of the way Liberians like to dress – wearing fashionable Western clothes and African attire, such as vai shirts and lappa suits.

Food in Sierra Leone is also very similar to ours in Liberia, with lots of rice, fufu, and soups, like cassava leaf soup. Everyone I met was amiable, hospitable, and generous, and, like us, they spoke many languages.

The markets, roads, homes, and buildings in

Freetown were all well-constructed and modern and everything was very well maintained. This made it easy for me to find my way around, and I made a lot of new friends while I lived there.

When I had been staying at the hotel for a month, I met a woman named Oretha. As we chatted, I learned she knew my friend Hawah.

"She's living right here in Freetown," Oretha told me. "I'll let her know you're here. I'm sure she'd love to see you. Where are you staying?" I told Oretha the name of my hotel, and she wasted no time at all getting in touch with Hawah. The very next day, my friend and her husband pulled up in front of the place where I was staying. They gave me a warm welcome and invited me to come and stay with them at their house. The prospect of being reunited with my friend delighted me. So, I immediately accepted their offer and checked out of the hotel. We all piled into their car, and they drove me to their place. I stayed with them for five months, and it was a wonderful time of peace and joy for me. After so many years of hardship, I revelled in their kindness and generosity.

Towards the end of my stay, I once again did my rounds at the markets, looking for bargains that I could sell back in Liberia. I bought some lovely ladies' handbags, smart men's shoes, and a variety of gorgeous clothes for men and women. I left Freetown with my bags filled to bursting.

When I got back to Monrovia, I went to my sister's

house. Although I enjoyed my time in Sierra Leone, Liberia will always be home to me, and it felt good to be surrounded by my family once more.

My sister was thrilled when she saw all the wonderful items I had purchased. She sold them all at the local market and used the money she earned to support the family. When I saw how much this small act of generosity and love meant to my sister and her family, I knew I had done the right thing.

Charles Taylor wins election

All the while, the politicians and warlords continued their struggle for power, with no regard for the country being ravaged beneath their feet.

From May to July 1996, the militia made a slow withdrawal from central Monrovia, although all factions kept contingency arms and personnel within the city.

In August, yet another peace agreement was signed – this time in Abuja, Nigeria. Signatories of the Abuja Accord agreed to disarmament and demobilisation of troops by 1997. Surprisingly, this accord appeared to hold and, despite the less-than-ideal circumstances, elections for the presidency and national assembly occurred simultaneously, as planned in July 1997.

Unsurprisingly, Charles Taylor won the presidential poll, taking seventy-five percent of the vote amidst widespread allegations of intimidation. His newly formed National Patriotic Party (NPP) took three-quarters of the legislative seats. Taylor's closest competitor, Ellen Sirleaf, garnered only ten percent of the vote.

Part 8

1996–2012

LOVE COMES CALLING

Phillip Harris

As the war slowly came to an end, many of the child soldiers who stalked the streets were being disarmed, and life in Monrovia once again reverted to some semblance of normalcy.

At the time, I lived in a flat with several other women, and we revelled in the newfound freedom of being able to go out without fearing for our lives. We would all pile into the car Marco Carto had given me and drive around the city, heading to the shops or the beach or a pub or restaurant, letting our hair down and enjoying ourselves – even if it was for just a little while.

On one of these outings, my friend Christiana insisted on introducing me to someone she knew among the UN peacekeeping forces.

"His name is Phillip Harris," she told me, a twinkle in her eye. "He's English, and I think you'll like him." I was sceptical, but I went along to please her.

The bar where we met was peppered with UN soldiers, who were all staying in a big hotel nearby. I purchased a glass of bright purple Vimto – a soft drink made from the juice of grapes, raspberries, and blackcurrants, flavoured with herbs and spices. It was all the rage amongst my group – when we weren't drinking beer. Once we had our drinks, Christiana scanned the room.

"Oh, there he is," she said, wriggling her fingers at a dapper gentleman sitting at a corner table. We made our way over to him. He stood up as we approached.

"Hi Phil," said Christiana. "This is my best friend, Rita. I was telling you about her last time we spoke." Phil smiled.

"Hi Christiana. Lovely to meet you, Rita," he said and reached out a hand towards me. I shook it gingerly. By this time, I was deeply suspicious of men, but something about Phillip intrigued me. He seemed more mature, gentler, and certainly less arrogant than the other men (mostly Americans) I had met up to that point.

Given the terrible conditions we were living under, I wondered what such a lovely man was doing in Liberia, and I asked him, "What brings you to Liberia?"

Slightly shocked at my directness, Phil gave me a wry smile and said, "I'm here as part of the UN team. We're working with the boy soldiers. Our goal is to disarm and deprogram them. We're trying to educate them and help them deal with their trauma, so that they can assimilate into normal society. It's very challenging, but also rewarding work."

"So, you're not a soldier, then?" I asked, incredulous.

"No, I'm a civilian. I work for the UN. In fact, not to brag or anything, but I'm actually the Chief of Aviation, which means I'm in charge of air safety and air operations."

We talked for a long time. During a lull in the conversation, Phillip asked, "Hey Rita, are you okay?"

He caught me off guard with that question. No one had asked me that since I was a child living in my uncle's house in Gardnersville. I felt the sting of tears in my eyes, and after trying to suppress them without any luck, I looked into his lovely, compassionate face and said, "No, Phil. I'm not okay at all." Then, despite my deep embarrassment, I started to cry.

Apologising to Phil, I tried desperately to get back in control of my emotions, but he only looked at me kindly and held out a clean handkerchief for me to dry my eyes with.

I thanked him, and he replied, "Bless you, my dear. It's going to be alright."

We talked some more, and as we did, I felt a tremendous sense of joy and relief at finally having met someone who seemed to be genuinely interested in me and my life.

When it was time to say goodnight and go home, I was reluctant to leave. I wondered if I would ever see this lovely man again. My fears were allayed when the very next day, Phillip called my friend and asked her if he could meet me for lunch.

We met at a restaurant, and once again, I felt that wonderful feeling of peace and joy in his presence. Phillip wanted to know all about my life in the village, and how I had survived during the war. I knew instinctively that I could trust this man, so I poured my heart out to him. At times, my story moved him to tears, and I could not believe the empathy and compassion he showed me. It reminded me of the Samaritan woman who met Jesus at the well, and how He showed her compassion when everyone else, including herself, judged her and shunned her.

At the end of the meal, Phil said, "Rita, thank you for sharing your story with me. You are a brave and resourceful woman, and I admire you a great deal."

I was speechless as I tried to process this. For an instant, I wondered whether there was some catch. Something he wanted from me, but I could not fathom what it could be. All the men I had met up to that point had only ever been interested in paying me to have sex with them. They never took the time, as Phil had done, to listen to my story. I never had to wonder what they wanted; they came right out and told me.

Phil had said nothing of the sort. He had treated me with nothing but respect, and he seemed genuine when he said that he liked me. I realised I was standing there in silence, and Phil was beginning to feel uncomfortable. So, I said, "I'm sorry, it's just that I'm not used to men treating me this way. I've never met anyone like you. I'm not used to a man simply wanting to enjoy my company. It's… Well, it's wonderful. I like you very much."

Phil asked me if there was anything I needed, and I told him we were desperately short of food. So, on the way home, he took me to buy some food and gave me extra money "for expenses". His generosity floored me.

When I got home, I showed the money to one of my friends.

"What did you have to do for him to get all that?" she asked.

"Nothing," I replied.

"Nothing? Really?" She was incredulous.

"Yep. He didn't even ask me to come up to his hotel room." I couldn't help being a little smug about it. My friend gaped at me. None of us had ever been treated this way by a man before, and while they were all happy for me, I could tell they were waiting, as I was, for the catch to become apparent.

Phillip was only in Liberia for a short amount of time. He had been in Western Sahara before and would soon move on to his next assignment. So, he wasted no time in courting me.

The day after our lunch date, he invited me up to his hotel room. I thought, "Oh well, it was nice while it lasted. Here come the demands." But he made no demands on me. Instead, he asked me if I would like to stay with him. I hesitated, unsure of what to say.

"You can stay for as long as you like," he assured me. So, I said yes.

Those first weeks with Phillip were amongst the happiest of my life. Revelling in each other's company, we spent as much time together as his schedule allowed. I had already shared a lot of my story with Phillip, and now, I wanted to know all about him – what his life had been like before he came to Liberia, what his family were like, and what had led him to join the UN and do the dangerous work he did.

He revealed himself to me as we lingered over sumptuous dinners at various restaurants, during long walks on the beach, and while unwinding together in the comfort of his hotel room.

Phillip's story

Born in the 1940s, in Abbotsbury, a village in Dorset, close to Chesil Beach, Phillip became fascinated by planes at an early age. He loved nothing more than watching them flying over his hometown.

His early fascination with aircraft blossomed into a career that started at Heathrow Airport and would eventually take him all over the world. Phillip specialised in aviation safety, and, while he was working in Singapore, the UN approached him with an offer to work for their Department of Peacekeeping Missions.

Phillip accepted, and his UN assignments took him far and wide from the world's leading cities to some of the most remote corners of the globe. During each tour of duty, Phil witnessed the worst of human behaviour, including an array of horrifying injuries and mutilations inflicted on innocent civilians, including women, children, and older adults.

Phil's team worked extensively with child soldiers, many of whom were traumatised, brainwashed, under the influence of alcohol and drugs, and carrying rifles that were taller than they were.

"Why do you do it then?" I asked, after he had told me how upsetting it was to see so much suffering.

"The people we rescue are the reason I love my job. I do it because I love seeing the looks on the faces of those whom we are able to save. Knowing that we make a real difference in people's lives makes it all worthwhile. The team and I, we don't dwell on the bad stuff. You wouldn't be able to carry on if you did that. Instead, we focus on the good we're doing. That's what gets us through."

The more I got to know more about Phillip, the deeper my feelings became for this wonderful man. And it wasn't long before I realised I had fallen in love with him. *Did he feel the same way about me?*

We'd only been together for a short time, and his work meant that he could be stationed elsewhere at any time. Phil had been just a couple weeks into his first contract in Liberia when we met, and as time flew by, I worried about where he would go next. *Was I getting caught up in something that would end up in heartbreak and disappointment?*

Phil's proposal

I did not have to worry for very long, as it turned out. Two weeks into our relationship, Phil invited me to a fancy hotel, called Hotel Africa, in Brewerville. While we were dining on a delicious meal and enjoying each other's company, he leaned across the table and took both my hands in both of his. Then he looked into my eyes and said, "Rita, will you do me the honour of being my wife?"

Initially, I didn't know how to react. My first instinct was to laugh out loud (I didn't though). It was just such a shock. No one had ever asked me that question before.

When Phil had said he wanted to help me, we were on firmer ground. I understood exactly what that meant. Or at least I thought I did. The friendship with mutual benefits we had cultivated up to this point had been hard enough to process, but love was something else altogether. All my encounters with men so far had been transactional. There was no love involved, and both sides had always known it.

But Phil was not like the other men I knew. Instead of always demanding, he was kind, sincere, and trustworthy. He took care of me – providing me with food, money, and a place to stay. And all the while, I knew he would not stay in Liberia. Soon enough, his work would take him away from me. I had made up my mind that this rare undemanding relationship would not – could not – last forever. Yet, over the past few months, we had grown closer. And now, here he was, telling me he loved me and asking me to marry him. I felt completely overwhelmed by it all.

Aside from the love I felt for my family and for Chris, I could honestly say I had never experienced love as an adult. This romantic love was a foreign concept to me. I knew I had strong feelings for Phil – complex, powerful feelings. Was that love? I did not know. I supposed it must be. Despite my doubts and confusion, Phil's gentle reassuring presence, and the love he showed to me, convinced me then, as it has every day since, that what we had was, and still is, true love.

So, instead of laughing, I clamped my hand over my mouth and stared at Phil in amazement. I looked into his eyes and examined the set of his face. His features were cast in a look of agonised ardour. I knew he was dead serious. I thought, Wow! This can't really be happening. Then I took a deep breath, calmed myself down and said, "Yes, Phil. I would love to be your wife."

We both laughed. The tension eased. Phil ordered a bottle of champagne, and we toasted our relationship and our future together. For that moment, all the worries and cares in my life seemed to lift and float away, and I was blissfully happy.

Phil has taught me so much about love over the long years of our marriage, and most of it by the shining example he sets in word and deed.

Phil meets my family

My family was thrilled when I brought Phil around to meet them.

"I can tell that he is a good man," my sister told me. "He's a godsend."

They were even more excited when Phil told them he would like to marry me and asked them for their blessing.

"We are so happy for you both. This is wonderful news," said my sister.

They sobered for a while when they realised exactly what my marriage to Phil would mean – that I would leave Liberia and would probably not see them all again for a very long time. But they adored and respected Phillip, and they accepted our marriage as part of God's plan. So, they cheered up again and shared in our joy.

"Even though we're all going to miss you terribly," my sister said, "it's good to know that you'll be safe and have someone to take care of you."

That was my family through and through – the most loving people in the world. Though we could not take them all with us, they did not resent me for leaving with Phil – far from it. They rejoiced in my good fortune and were genuinely glad that someone had grabbed my hand and saved my life.

Our wedding

Phil had received news that his next assignment would be in Monrovia, and he wanted me to travel there with him as his wife. So, we set the wedding date for a week after receiving my family's blessing.

We had a traditional wedding, surrounded by our friends and my family. Phil and I both wore traditional African attire made of brightly coloured lappa cloth, and we had beans tied around our necks. It was a beautiful day, and everyone danced and shared some refreshments after the ceremony.

During the speeches, Phil expressed his gratitude to my family for allowing him to marry me and promised them we would return to Liberia to see them when the crisis was over. Phil's family, being in England, could not travel to Liberia because of the crisis. So, unfortunately, they could not attend the wedding. But we made up for this with a second wedding when we eventually made our way to England about six months later.

There was no time for a honeymoon, as Phil was due in Morocco right away. So, we said our goodbyes, dried our tears, and headed off on a new life of travel and adventure together.

A prophecy fulfilled

I left Liberia with Phillip on 31 August 1997. Though I was sad to say goodbye to my friends and family, I knew I was fulfilling the destiny that my grandmother had foretold all those years ago in my home village of Jeadepo. We had been sitting beside the fire talking about our dreams of the future when Grandma had told me, "God has blessed you with travelling grace. You will travel from country to country in your lifetime, and you will eventually live in a white race country." Now, this prophecy had come to pass.

After marrying Phil, I travelled to many African and European countries and lived in exotic places all around the world.

Meeting Phillip's family

Phil and I had been married for six months when, one evening over dinner, he cleared his throat and said, "How would you like to meet my mother?"

"I'd love to," I said, grinning.

"Good. It's settled then," he said and clinked glasses with me. "We're bound for England."

So, we packed up our things in Morocco, and I readied myself to meet my in-laws. Though I felt a little nervous about meeting Phil's family, I was sure that they must be lovely people since they had such a wonderful son. In the short time we'd been married, Phil had already taught me what unconditional love and kindness looked like, and I was certain that God sent him as a gift just for me. So, I drew on the strength of that knowledge as we made our way to Reading, where Phil's mum Phyllis lived.

As soon as she opened the door and showed us into her home, I realised any fears I'd had were completely unfounded. Phyllis was such a warm and affectionate person who simply radiated positive energy. She welcomed me with open arms.

"I'm so very pleased to meet you, Rita," she said. "Welcome to England and welcome to our home."

I thanked her, and from that moment on, Phyllis and I have shared a special bond. She has been a wonderful role model and also a mother to me. She taught me so much about English culture and their way of life. Phyllis also introduced me to classical music, which was her favourite type of music, and I found I enjoyed it very much. We went on shopping trips many times and made wonderful memories together. She also taught me a lot about Phil – what he liked and didn't like, and other things that would help me build a strong relationship with her son.

She took me around and proudly introduced me to her neighbours as her daughter-in-law, and every one of them enfolded me in so much love and affection that I felt I would burst with joy. For the first time since those carefree days in Jeadepo, I felt I was once again surrounded by loving people who accepted me unconditionally.

While we were staying in Reading, Phil's two sons, Stuart and Carl, came to the house to meet me. They too, were very warm, welcoming, and kind to me. We all got along so well and had wonderful times, making treasured memories. The boys have always accepted and respected me and treated me with love and affection. They make me feel as though I am the most important woman on earth. When people see how much these two young men love and appreciate me, they all say it is hard to believe we are not blood relatives. I am forever grateful to God that I have such good and lasting relationships with everyone in Phil's family.

Maureen

A few months later, around December 1997, Phil mentioned that his ex-wife Maureen, whom he still had an amicable relationship with, was visiting the UK from Spain, and that he would like me to meet her. I agreed, and we went to Tadley, where Maureen was staying with her mother. I was even more nervous meeting Maureen than I had been meeting Phil's family. But once again, I was pleasantly surprised. Maureen was just as warm and welcoming as the rest of Phil's family. She accepted me straightaway, and I could tell her joy at meeting me was genuine.

Maureen is a very intelligent woman, and it was a pleasure chatting with her. I could tell that she was truly happy for Phil and me, and I caught not the slightest hint of jealousy in her response to me. When we left, she encouraged us to visit her home in Spain whenever we could arrange it.

Life with Phil

During the early years of our marriage, I learned more about Phillip. His life had been one of adventure, but also tremendous challenge and trauma. One thing is certain – it had never been dull. He had lived all over the world, seen many amazing things and met lots of interesting people. Now that I would accompany him on his adventures, I was filled with excitement to see the wider world.

The first place we lived in after leaving Liberia was Morocco. We had only been there for a year when Phillip was sent to Angola. I followed him, and while we were there, I fell pregnant. For the sake of our baby, we decided it was best for me to go to New York in the final months of my pregnancy. So, I went to stay with one of my aunts. There, I gave birth to a healthy baby boy, whom we named Shaun.

Since those early days of childhood when I played mother to my corn dolls, there was never a time in my life when I did not want to be a mother. And though his birth brought back some painful memories of the days when I had been compelled to give up my first son, I was thrilled beyond belief as I held my newborn baby in my arms. I had always wanted more children, and Shaun's arrival was one of the best things that have ever happened to me.

The joy I felt at Shaun's birth was immense. My heart felt as if it would burst out of my chest, and by the look on his face, and the tender way he held our baby, I knew Phillip felt the same way. Shaun was truly a blessing from God and the start of a whole new life for both of us.

Later that year, Phil was stationed in Sierra Leone, and I went with him, carrying our infant son. In those days, I lived wherever Phillip was stationed. I took care of our son, cooked meals, and managed the household while he worked. Though we lived off-base, the UN compounds had on-site cafeterias where I would meet up with Phillip for lunch.

As Shaun grew older, he attended various UN schools, and I took care of him when he came home. This was the norm for most families of UN workers. Much like the military families, we formed a supportive network while our menfolk were away working in dangerous situations.

Learning English from Phyllis

We stayed in Africa for three years, at which point Phillip suggested that Shaun and I should go back to the UK to live with Phyllis for a while. This would give Shaun and me the opportunity to improve our English skills and absorb some of the British culture.

Although I had learned some English at school, my mother tongue was Grebo. My English was not as proficient as it should be if I were to assimilate into society when we were stationed in English-speaking countries.

Phyllis was a lovely woman, and we formed a close bond. I thoroughly enjoyed my time in England with her. Besides helping me to improve my English, she also taught me other skills, such as how to cook English food, eat with a knife and fork, and use the correct posture. Long after our three-year sojourn in England was over, I often returned to England for visits, staying for a couple of months each time before going back to my life with Phil.

THOUGH YOU SLAY ME

Travelling grace

My grandma had been right – God had indeed blessed me with travelling grace. Travel has been (and will always be) in my blood. I recall dreaming about planes when I was little. In one dream I remember vividly, the plane landed on the river in our village.

Particularly in the early years of our marriage, I spent a lot of time travelling around the world with Phil. During that time, I saw so many amazing places and people and tried so many wonderful kinds of cuisine. It was truly eye-opening to see how other people lived. As a young girl back in Jeadepo, I would never have believed it possible that my dreams of travel would come true.

Singapore was far and away my favourite place to live. I loved visiting the food halls and shopping malls, and I marvelled at how immaculate everything was. The wide range of Asian cuisine on offer was especially enticing, and I loved trying the different dishes. Within a short time, I developed a particular fondness for Singapore noodles.

Norway also stood out to me as a special place. I loved how peaceful it was, and how tidy everything was – even in the cities. The Norwegian people were so friendly, and I especially loved being so close to nature all the time. I discovered a passion for hiking in the Norwegian mountains and spent many happy days absorbing the beautiful surroundings of the fjords and the forests.

It was (and possibly still is) common in Norway for people to head out into nature before they went into work.

This practice seemed to make a difference, as I noticed Norwegians seemed to be far less stressed than people in other countries I visited. Being a foodie, I found Norway a little disappointing, but only because I couldn't help comparing Norwegian cuisine to the amazing food I had enjoyed in Singapore.

One place I would still love to see is Antarctica. The thought of the beauty and serenity I might find there, and the glory of the southern lights fills me with awe.

Chris

When Phil told me we were moving to Lebanon, I was overjoyed because it meant I could reconnect with my eldest son, Christopher, who was over there studying IT. I loved having the opportunity to establish a stronger bond with him.

Being separated from him when he was a baby had been hard, although not as traumatic as you might think. In our culture, many children are raised by their aunts and uncles, or by their grandparents, just as I had been. Instead of individual family units, we all formed part of a single, close-knit wider family group. No one was excluded, and we were all a part of each other's lives. So, our situation was nothing unusual.

Under normal circumstances, Chris and I would have been able to spend time with each other and form close bonds with each other over the years. But the war drove us apart, severing the ties that would normally have formed. We had started to get to know each other a little during the time I lived with my sister's family in Monrovia, but back then he still thought of me as his aunty. Now that he was seventeen, and we were both living in Lebanon, I could reconnect with him – this time as his mother. It took a few years, but when he finally called me Mum, I thought my heart would burst with joy and love.

Nowadays, we spend hours talking to each other on the phone. I am very proud of him. He has grown into a handsome man with good Christian values. When he completed his studies, Chris went back to Liberia to work in the government fire service. He has been blessed with all the things I wished for him and his life.

Homesickness

I loved my new life travelling the world with Phil. I was happy in my marriage and grateful that I could send money back home. Yet, I missed my family terribly, and I longed to see them again. I harboured a secret hope that conditions in the country would improve so I could return to Liberia someday.

Sometimes, when feelings of despair and homesickness threatened to overwhelm me, it felt as though there were vultures tearing at the flesh of my heart, leaving it raw and bleeding. On these occasions, even the small challenges I faced each day seemed insurmountable.

The memories I carried from my childhood in

the village somehow persisted. I recalled with longing the peaceful community of people sitting outside, chatting and eating together, bound by bonds of love and friendship. The harmonious culture I had been raised in permeated throughout Liberian society, and I recognised it within all the different communities I lived in during the war.

Liberians are tough-minded. We have an uncanny knack of being able to keep smiling and stay positive. The close-knit community made up of my friends and relatives helped me survive during the most horrific times. No matter how poor, starving, and terrified we were, we all cared for one another. Even during the worst days of the civil war, we supported each other and buoyed one another up with small acts of kindness. We did not stand on ceremony, waiting to be invited over; we went into one another's houses, offering help and comfort. Sometimes, all we could offer was a sympathetic ear and a shoulder to cry on, but that never stopped us. We gave what we could, shared what we had and were all much better for it.

There's no denying that the war left ugly scars on our souls. We were traumatised by all we had seen and done and lived through, and we all have a lot to process. But the hardships we went through forged lifelong friendships. And I'm still in touch with many of the women I lived with during the war.

Meanwhile, my Aunty Jessica, who lives in the US, worked hard to get my family out of Liberia, and we were relieved when, eventually, the UN agreed to grant them refugee status, which allowed them to enter and live in various parts of the world.

Knowing that God sent Phil to rescue me, and that He has a plan for my life was (and still is) an immense comfort to me. And I tried to forget about the devastation and the war by focusing on the here-and-now and making the best life I could for our little family.

A global community

People often ask me whether I experienced racism or discrimination during my travels, and I can honestly say that this was never an issue. Wherever I went, I was welcomed by one and all as though I was an old friend or family member. I experienced no prejudice based on my skin colour, and I never felt there was anywhere I couldn't go or anything I could not do because I was African.

Similarly, I never experienced much religious tension. Phillip and I are both Christians, and our faith is very important to us. Yet, we had no difficulties when we were stationed in Muslim countries.

When we lived in the Western Sahara, I regularly ate, drank, and socialised with Muslim women with no recriminations. We simply accepted each other and lived in harmony. When we went to weddings or parties, I would dress in Moroccan clothing – not because I had to, but out of choice. I ate couscous and danced with those around me, feeling just as at home as if I had grown up there. Everywhere we visited, we made lasting friendships, and we still keep in touch to this day.

Whenever Phillip worked at the UN headquarters in New York, we based ourselves in Philadelphia, as I wasn't keen on New York City. This meant Phillip had to commute two hours each way, but he felt that was worth it since we both loved Philadelphia. As with so many other places I've been, I made friends easily, and my friends always loved Phillip. Our friends became like family.

Life on UN bases

Being the wife of a UN employee was not always easy. Sometimes I could not go with Phil when he went on missions, particularly into dangerous areas. In those times, I would have to remain behind and pray for his safety while waiting for him to return. I did my best to have faith and busied myself with taking care of my children. The support of other wives in the UN compounds was invaluable during such times.

While living on UN bases, I had to host and attend parties, often with high-ranking people on the guest list. At one such party, we even hosted the British Ambassador. I thoroughly enjoyed this part of my life, as I have always been sociable and friendly, and loved making things beautiful and special for our guests.

A little push

Phil came from a different, more traditional era than I had. Men of Phil's generation believed it was normal, even expected, for a man to take care of and provide for his wife, while she stayed at home and raised the family. As Shaun put it, 'Dad is old school', meaning that Phil was happy for me to stay at home. So, throughout the early part of our marriage, Phil gave me an allowance that made it possible for me to stay at home and take care of Shaun.

Being a wife and a mother certainly was a full-time job, and at first, I was grateful for the support. It gave me the time and space I needed to heal and recover from the ordeals I had faced during the war. I cannot describe how good it felt not to be constantly under financial pressure – knowing that there would always be a roof over our heads, clothes on our backs and food on our plates – especially after the horrors of my twenties.

But as Shaun got older and needed me less often, I worried I might get too dependent on Phil. I am much younger than Phil and come from a different generation where everyone does their bit and earns their own wage. With this background, I could not help feeling that Phil was spoiling me, and that perhaps he was being a bit over-protective.

Also, as my duties as a mother diminished, I couldn't shake the feeling that I was being lazy. I kept waiting for Phil to push me to do more with my brains and my talents, but he never did. Eventually, I realised that he wasn't going to push me – I needed to push myself.

Time to settle down

When Shaun reached high school age, we agreed he needed stability and a good education. It was time for us to find a more permanent home base where we could put down roots. So, in 2007, Shaun and I settled down in Manchester. Phil was still in Lebanon and would continue to travel for his job, but digital communications were improving, and this made keeping in touch a lot easier – even when we were in different countries.

With my travelling days over, and Shaun reaching an age when he was more independent, I realised the time had come for me to give myself that push. I wanted to make my own money, so I could put something aside to help my family. I knew I had a lot to offer, and I started looking at employment options.

Allergic to books

I soon realised that before I could get a job, I needed to spend some time furthering my education. This was not a simple decision as, sadly, my school days had left me with an intense dislike of books and learning. The thought of any kind of reading or writing terrified me. I kept having flashbacks of my time at school when everyone from teachers to relatives tried in vain to get me to knuckle down and persevere with my studies. Despite their encouragement, I had always hated studying – all that sitting still in one place for hours always made me feel like I had to get up and do something.

THOUGH YOU SLAY ME

In the end, I went ahead and enrolled anyway. So, while Shaun attended Bury Grammar, an all-boys private school in the northern part of the city, I took a course in childcare at Manchester College.

The nagging belief that I was hopeless at anything academic plagued me all the time while I tried to complete the course. Eventually, I spoke to my teacher about my misgivings. She was very supportive and understanding. She took the time to explain everything to me in detail and reassured me that the test wouldn't involve too much writing – instead it would be multiple choice.

When the time came for me to take the test, my self-confidence was still fragile. I braced myself, said a quick prayer and went in. I shook with nerves, and the paper crinkled beneath my sweaty hand as I marked off the answers on my multiple-choice answer sheet. All the while, I thought I was simply guessing, but it turned out later that I had not been guessing, and in fact, I had got the merit I had been aiming for in my final exam. I whooped in celebration when I saw the results, tears of joy and relief streaming down my face. Nevertheless, it didn't stop Shaun from cheekily suggesting that I was "allergic to books".

Although I did not relish studying, God showered His grace upon me, blessing me with a spirit of humility and a love of people, along with the energy, passion, and determination to do my best and achieve my goals in life.

While I believe that education is essential, especially in today's world, I also recognise that the fulfilment of one's destiny does not solely depend on your intellectual capability. Instead, the quality of a person's character determines his or her success in life. We are all beneficiaries of God's grace, and when we rely on Him, exercise self-discipline, and stay committed to our calling, we will come to a place of fulfilment in our lives.

Working as a carer

Once qualified, I found a job escorting children with disabilities to school. This meant that occasionally Shaun had to take a taxi to his school, if my schedule clashed with his, but that was not a problem for us financially.

I adored my job, which suited my maternal, caring personality. The positive energy and enthusiasm of the children I worked with was a healing balm to my soul. I soaked up their happy, carefree vibes, and they made me feel a renewed love for life. Kindness and patience come naturally to me, and I did my best to truly connect with each child – even when they had a difficult time communicating. They loved and respected me in return – despite my imperfect English language skills. The children were very affectionate and responded well to hugs.

Often, I comforted children with Down's Syndrome or autism, holding them against my chest if they started having an episode and soothing them until they calmed down. I also forged strong relationships with the children's parents, who were grateful for the love and acceptance I showed towards their children. It was a very rewarding role where I felt I was doing essential work.

When that role ended, I wanted to try a new job and experience new things. So, I got a job in a care home, tending to the needs of people at the other end of the age spectrum. I loved taking care of people, and I enjoyed the hands-on practicalities of helping those with complex needs. However, there was still paperwork involved, and being "allergic to books", I did my best to avoid it. I can still remember praying that an elderly lady wouldn't pass away, simply so that I would not have to write an extra report about it.

Regardless of my aversion to paperwork, writing up a report at the end of each shift was a requirement of the job and had to be done, whether I liked it or not. Fortunately for me, a very kind Pakistani lady who also worked in the home offered to help me out. She was an incredible source of support, but she couldn't do it all the time. So, at the end of every shift, there was this awful thing I had to do, and it really diminished my enjoyment of the job.

To make matters worse, I worked the night shift, and with Phil abroad, that meant Shaun would be left alone at home most nights. For a while, we had a friend come over to take care of Shaun in the evenings, but it wasn't a long-term solution. In the end, I realised it was not the right job for me, and I left.

Phillip was as supportive of my decision to leave as he had been of my decision to study and to work. He never stopped me from trying my hand at different jobs once Shaun was old enough. Phil was always happy for me to make a go of it, and he made it clear that he was proud of me, no matter what I did. He didn't push me too hard. I knew he loved me, and he never wanted me to feel pressured. I thanked God for Phil's steady, supportive nature, and his constant reassurance to me that everything would be fine, that he would take care of me and there was nothing to worry about.

Itchy feet

Overall, I found settling down in one place challenging, especially after having been on the move for so long. Although at first the idea of travelling to new countries had been intimidating, I had never minded living out of a suitcase, as some people seemed to. And over time, my confidence had improved. All those parties, rubbing shoulders with important people, had made me realise I was smart, friendly, outgoing, and a good conversationalist. I was certain that I could hold my own wherever we went. Also, I had gotten a taste for the fast-paced life of a UN wife – always meeting new people, seeing new places and experiencing new things – not to mention trying out different cuisine. Now those days were all over; I found it hard to settle down. As a result, after a few years of living in Manchester, I felt restless. I longed for a change of scenery.

In 2012, I got my wish. We were moving again, and even though it was only to another city in the UK, I felt the old excitement returning. This time, we moved to the beautiful town of Devon, where we lived in a large farmhouse in the heart of the countryside. I rekindled my love of hiking, and we spent many happy hours taking long walks and enjoying the outdoors. We were close to Cornwall and the ocean, and it felt amazing to be back in touch with nature again – even if it meant we were miles away from anywhere and had to rely heavily on our car.

Finding my niche

I got a job as a housekeeper for a family in Devon. After one very enjoyable year, I realised that this was my true calling. I really love cleaning. In the same way that I excelled at taking care of people, I also had a natural gift for cleaning. There's nothing about it I don't like. I enjoy the detail involved in making sure you cover all areas. You can't miss anything in a deep clean, and I appreciate the rigour and the challenge that comes with that.

Part 9

2013–2023

A FORTUNATE LIFE

The Isle of Wight

By the time Phil retired from his role at the UN, we had already been living in Devon for a few years. So, we settled on the Isle of Wight, a boat ride away from the busy shipping city of Portsmouth.

Though I have always been proud of Phil and the work he does, his job was very dangerous, and when he retired, I could finally breathe a sigh of relief, knowing that he would be home safe and sound.

In retirement, Phil has been free to indulge his love of cooking, which means the household chores fell neatly into two spheres, with Phil doing the cooking he loves, and me doing the cleaning that I enjoy. That's still the way we do it.

Doing what I love

Shortly after moving to the Isle of Wight, I took a cleaning job at a local holiday resort, and I've thrived in this environment. Though I work six days a week, only taking Sundays off, I enjoy my job so much that it doesn't feel like a burden at all. I take immense pride in my work. I have always enjoyed working with my hands more than anything else, and I find cleaning very satisfying as you can see the results of your labour immediately.

Attention to detail is important in cleaning – nothing should be ignored or left undone. It's important to me that each room is a better place for my being in it, and at the end of each day, I celebrate a job well done.

I always pray before I head into work, asking God to ensure that everything goes smoothly, and I have a fantastic day. And my prayers always seem to get answered, as there have been very few bad days and I've never had any difficult colleagues.

Smiling and staying upbeat are crucial in my line of work. I try to remain on good terms with everyone at the resort – staff and guests. Fortunately, I'm naturally amenable and good-humoured, which makes this easy. I was always taught to be respectful and humble, and I try to be a positive presence in the lives of those around me. As a result, I've forged strong relationships with my colleagues and our guests at the Seaview Holiday Resort.

Not one instance of prejudice or racism

As my grandma predicted, I am a Black woman living in a European country, surrounded predominantly by White people. And yet, I have experienced none of the discrimination or isolation that I feared might be an issue. People might expect that I would be the object of a certain amount of prejudice and racism. But this is not the case at all.

In all the years I've worked at Seaview, I have never experienced even one instance of racism or discrimination from the guests or my colleagues and bosses.

I thank God daily for the tremendous team of people I work with. I'm very fortunate to have supportive and friendly colleagues. My bosses are always positive and kind, and I show my appreciation for their kindness through the willingness and humility I show towards them. We are like one big, happy family. We treat each other with mutual care and respect. I am proud and grateful to be an employee at this wonderful resort.

A loving community

This sense of unconditional acceptance permeates through our entire community. Even in the casual and part-time jobs I do in Seaview Village, I'm treated with respect and dignity. I have always been given the opportunities and support I needed and desired.

England and her people have treated me with kindness, generosity, gentleness, decency, and affection. Her people have accepted and welcomed me unconditionally. God bless England! May her days be filled with the love and joy of Christ Jesus.

My husband – a true gentleman

My husband is a constant blessing to me. His unconditional love and affection keep me going each day. I am blessed to have a loving gentleman in my life. I often tell him, "God bless the day your mother bore you." To which he responds with a smile before drawing me into a warm embrace.

In fact, Phil's naturally warm nature and positive outlook make it easy to forget that he has endured his fair share of trauma. Long periods spent in war zones have left him with post-traumatic stress disorder (PTSD) and high blood pressure that require constant management with help from medical professionals. These issues have affected Phil's life in many ways. He cannot even enjoy the simple pleasure of watching a movie or a show on television, as he never knows whether it may contain scenes that will trigger his PTSD and elevate his blood pressure.

Marriage

We both carry deep wounds from the horrors we have lived through and, though we try to understand and support each other, sometimes the age gap between us and the different ways we deal with our past traumas can make married life challenging. Sometimes, Phillip wants to be calm and rest, while I want to be up and dancing.

However, our faith in God and the love we have for each other helps us to overcome our differences and keep on supporting each other. And in the end, that's what matters.

THOUGH YOU SLAY ME

To make our happy home life complete, we have been blessed with four beautiful boys: Chris (mine), Shaun (ours), Stuart and Carl (Phil's).

Family

Both Phil and I value family highly, and as a blended family, we are especially grateful to have superb close-knit relationships with all our boys.

We are also thankful that all our sons share our faith. Whenever they faced challenges in life, we always encouraged them to express their emotions, rather than bottling up their feelings, and to pray and trust in God to take care of all their needs. For instance, I suggested to Shaun that he pray before his job interview. He did and got the job, which was further proof to me that prayers are answered.

My boys have grown into happy, successful adults. I was always proud that Shaun and Christopher are so smart and hard-working, and so much happier at school than I ever was. They were both good at art. Christopher is particularly good at drawing faces, and Shaun excels at photography, a subject he later studied. Christopher continues to do well at his government job in Liberia, and Shaun works for Apple in the UK. Their happiness and success mean the world to me.

Faith

Our shared faith is also deeply important to us. Phillip and I were raised in Christian homes. We were always told that prayers would be answered, and that prayer could get you through hard times. Many times along our journey, we have found that praying together brings us great comfort. Finding places to worship while we travelled wasn't always easy; although we sometimes found churches in the most unexpected places, such as in the Western Sahara, which was, and still is, predominantly Islamic.

We moved onto the Isle of Wight during the COVID-19 pandemic when the churches were shut, but thanks to modern technology, we could attend Bible study via Zoom. It's good to know that God is always present, regardless of which building we might be worshipping in. Now that the epidemic is over, we worship at the Church of England, where we have been accepted wholeheartedly. We enjoy wonderful fellowship with this amazing bunch of Christian people.

I thank God for the church and its people, and I'm proud to be a member of this incredible congregation. They have provided unwavering support in every area of my life, including helping me to grow in the spirit and love of God, helping me to align my life with the purpose and the will of God, teaching me to live a life of moral standards, helping with material aids for my charitable organisations, and so much more.

God truly is faithful and just, and the supplier of all our needs. I have never doubted Him, and He has never let me down. Looking back on my life and the many times He has saved me; I am convinced that nothing is impossible for Him. I often thank Him and ask Him for help, and I have sensed His presence even in the most difficult and traumatic moments of my life. He has helped me even when I haven't been aware of it. My whole life is living proof of that.

I am thankful every morning that I am alive, and my hopes are rooted in Him. He guides Phil and me every day, and I want people to know that. All we have to do is to be wise enough to be open to His guidance. As the Scriptures say, we need to have "ears to hear" His words, and a "mouth to speak" of His goodness towards us.

Thoughts of home

Life might be peaceful and satisfying for me these days, but I still experience a lot of powerful emotions when I think about where I came from. I'm very grateful for the life I have, but deep down, I feel that I've never fully stopped being that girl who slept on the floor in a war zone and didn't see a disposable menstrual pad until she was an adult. I found them strange and uncomfortable at first, and I still find it very odd that something so wasteful can be easily bought at our local supermarket. It's humbling to think about that.

It upsets me when I think about all the Liberian people have gone through, and how much fighting and evil still exists in the world – despite the remarkable work done by people like my husband, who labour, day and night, to get ordinary people like me out of terrible situations.

Despite all the years of suffering, Liberia will always hold a special place in my heart. I was born there, and it will always be "home" to me.

There is so much that I miss about Liberia – the white sandy beaches, surfable waves, uninhabited islands, stunning wildlife, immense waterfalls, and bustling markets and cities, not to mention the hot, dry climate with none of the humidity found in other parts of the world.

I cherish the memories I have of the friends and family whose love surrounded me throughout my childhood. And thoughts of my grandparents are always tinged with equal parts joy and pain.

God's plan

No matter how bad things got for me during the war, I never gave in to despair because I knew in my heart that God had a plan and a purpose for my life. He is true to His Word, and His faithfulness is eternal. So, I rose every morning, and I looked outside my window at the rising sun, and I reminded myself that I could draw on God's power, that He would recharge me and keep me going. My faith helped me to keep on trying to survive and never give up – even when my spirits were low, my body weak and my mental state in disarray.

We can never be certain of the circumstances that await us in life, but if we have faith in Him, we will be able to keep our spirits up, no matter what befalls us.

Hopes and regrets

Sometimes, when I get homesick, I think that if I could, I would return to my life in the village in a heartbeat. Life was simple, and I never had to worry about a thing. We had no bills to pay, so money was not a problem. We knew that as long as our crops flourished, the creek gave us water, and the fire gave us heat, we had everything we needed. Each night at story time, I wanted nothing more than for those carefree days to last forever.

But perhaps I was always meant to leave Liberia.

My grandmother often used to comment on how I had lighter skin than my sister or cousins, sometimes jokingly calling me "white lady". She also accurately predicted that I would travel and live in a "white man's country" – something my mother almost had the chance to do, but never did.

When I met Phillip for the first time, I could not shake the feeling that this was part of God's plan, and it was always meant to happen. I felt that in some strange way, we had known each other all our lives.

Since leaving my homeland, I have had to go through a long and painful healing process, which left me forever changed, but also wiser and ready to start afresh.

I also wish that my younger self had been a little wiser. I would love to go back in time and tell the school-age Rita to value education a lot more. I would also like to tell the adult Rita to go back to school much sooner. A good education is the key to success.

But life is long, and despite my regrets, I have so many big hopes for the future. Since I can't go back and change the past, I have decided to focus on making a difference to the lives of children in Liberia. I am working hard to make better standards of education accessible to them. To this end, I've set up a non-government organisation (NGO) that gives Liberian children the help they need to cope at school.

Closer to home, I hope that my own children will enjoy success and prosperity and that they will continue to be well-mannered and caring at the same time.

For myself, I hope I will enjoy a long life. I'm excited by the thought of having grandchildren and maybe even great-grandchildren whom I'll one day get to meet. I also hope to grow wiser and more patient as I grow older.

Keeping my word

I kept my promise to Ma Fanta, the brave, compassionate, wonderful lady who saved my life and became my second mother. I have made the village of Gbatala my home now, and it always will be – just as Ma Fanta said it would be. I built a house there, and true to my word, I visit once a year.

Staying in Gbatala gives me the opportunity to reconnect with my people and my heritage, and while I'm there, I provide as much help as I can to those in need.

I have also set up a charitable organisation in Gbatala that runs programs to help people living in poverty and those suffering with disabilities and disease to live better, healthier and happier lives.

Finding joy in the little things

Having had so many huge events and massive upheavals in my life, I often find that now it's the small things in life that bring the most joy. I love the outdoors and enjoy staying fit by hiking and running whenever I can. Listening to classical music helps me relax at the end of a long day.

I also love to watch rugby, and I'm a big fan of the English rugby team. So much so that I had their rose emblem tattooed to my arm to mark my fortieth birthday.

In my life, I've been privileged to travel widely, and whenever we arrived in a new country, I purchased a fridge magnet as a souvenir. Our fridge is absolutely covered in them – even if a few have gone missing over the years.

Looking at them and remembering the wonderful adventures I've had helps to calm the feelings of restlessness I get from time to time.

Lessons learned

Life has taught me some harsh lessons, and I've had to guard my heart against bitterness, resentment, and negativity. I try to look past these negative attitudes in others, giving them the benefit of the doubt, and trying to understand where they are coming from before discounting them or shutting them out.

In doing so, I've noticed that, most often, these people are hurting deep down. They may say that they are okay, but, in fact, they are not.

I try to respond by being kind, humble, and positive, lending a sympathetic ear, and providing a shoulder to cry on. This makes a big difference, in most cases. There are some people who revel in negativity, though, and I've learned to let them go.

We all need to care for each other and talk to each other more. I've met a lot of people from so many places, and I've noticed that deep down we are all the same.

If we all tried to leave the world a better place than it was when we entered it, what a wonderful world it would be!

EPILOGUE

Lament for Liberia

Oh, Mama Liberia, where are those long-forgotten days, the days of our glory, the days of sunshine, the days of love and loyalty for the country? When I wake up and look outside my widow, all I see is the devastation of my people. No one seems to care about each other anymore. Everyone seems to be out for themselves these days. Liberians, where is the love of liberty that once united us? Has the war dulled our memories? Has it robbed us of our ability to care for our country, for each other, for our children?

Poverty

The Republic of Liberia covers around forty-three thousand square miles and sustains a population of approximately five million inhabitants. Although rich in fertile soil and natural resources, including gold, diamonds, iron ore, rubber, and palm oil, almost two decades of civil war have crippled the country. As a result, a large percentage of people in Liberia live in abject poverty, deprived of even the most fundamental requirements for survival, including food, clean water, shelter, sanitation, and access to basic health care.

While our leaders enjoy life, fill their bellies, and send their children to the best schools, the people of Liberia struggle to feed our families and are forced to commit loathsome acts just to survive.

According to the 2022 Global Hunger Index, food insecurity in the country is at an all-time low. Liberia ranked one hundred and thirteen out of the one hundred and twenty-one countries with sufficient data to calculate 2022 GHI scores. The score of thirty-two point four (32.4) indicates a serious level of hunger. This figure has declined steadily since the year 2000, when it was at forty-eight point two (48.2).

So many of us have been displaced by the fighting and no longer have homes to go to. We are living in the streets or in ghettos surrounded by drugs, prostitution, and violence. Our family units are disintegrating because of the hardships we all face on a daily basis, tensions have been running high for so long, we seem always to be poised on a knife-edge, on the brink of a fresh outbreak of civil unrest. Violence is a daily occurrence.

Commodities prices continue to rise, making it more difficult for the man-in-the-street to provide for his family. Ordinary people cannot afford medical treatment and are denied admission to hospitals and medical facilities around the country.

The hardships we have endured and continue to bear have left us dispirited, disillusioned and despondent.

Robbed of our dignity, we feel unworthy and unable to make the right decisions. We have been tempted and, in too many cases, forced into making all sorts of bad choices just to survive – selling sexual favours to have food to eat, or turning our children out onto the streets because we cannot feed them. And we have suffered the consequences of those choices.

The civil war may be over, but the economic war we are engaged in right now is just as deadly. During the war, the various factions, including the AFL, used food and poverty as tactics to win territory and gain power. Today, those in power take care only of themselves and their own families, without giving a thought to the masses living in squalor.

According to a recent report written by Liberia Country Economist Gweh Gaye Tarwo,

> *Liberia human capital outcomes are amongst the worst in the world, largely due to slow progress in education and health. [sic] The Liberian Government has made some strides in these sectors, but more can be done.*

Education disaster

Poverty is driving us to send our children to work, rather than sending them to school, and those who go to school do so with empty bellies that make it hard to concentrate. Instead of being educated and prepared as future leaders who will restore this country to greatness, our young people are lost to drugs, crime, violence, and the sex trade. Meanwhile, our young women are forced into early marriages simply because we cannot afford to feed them.

The crumbling school buildings, lack of resources and dearth of teachers testify to just how much the education system has broken down. There is no money to rebuild or even employ teachers to educate our young people. At present, the government does not provide subsidies, and neither does it monitor academic institutions.

To make matters worse, every day countless children simply disappear without a trace, only to be found dead in a field or swamp or never to be seen again. And the police cannot find the perpetrators and bring them to justice. Who will protect our little ones? Liberia, your future is being destroyed!

Corruption

Corruption has become a way of life in Liberia, instead of being a cause for nationwide concern. It should be considered the enemy of the state, as it undermines peace and stability and hinders the growth and development of the country.

Even in our schools, we see corruption, immorality, and unethical practices thriving. Bribery is the order of the day, and some teachers even ask students for sex in order to secure passing grades. Once again, our young girls and women are suffering at the hands of unscrupulous men, who show not the slightest concern for the damage they are doing to these innocent youngsters.

Sadly, students see this type of arrangement as an easy way to ensure their path through the education system, and as a result, they refuse to study. Many scholars also use drugs on school campuses, with no regard for the negative impact these substances have on their mental and physical health.

Drug addiction

Harmful substance abuse is rife in post-war Liberia, affecting the lives of many young Liberians. Drug addiction negatively affects their belief systems, emotions, and decision-making abilities.

Studies have revealed several risk factors for drug addiction amongst Liberian youth, including the psychological consequences of witnessing and participating in acts of violence, peer, or family pressure, separation from families during the war, dealing with the effects of poverty, lack of education, and unemployment.

Some drug dependency is rooted in the war where child soldiers and other young people were drugged in order to embolden them and turn them into fighting machines. High rates of PTSD and depression, and continued family and community violence also contribute to the high levels of substance abuse across the country. Corruption, underfunding, an overburdened justice system, and the many challenges involved in policing drug distribution, possession, and use are amongst the contributing factors in this complex scenario.

Drug addiction has had serious consequences for Liberian young people and the country as a whole. It has exacerbated the physical and mental health issues (PTSD, psychosis, paranoia) left by the war and has detrimental effects on society, including isolation from the family unit, disinterest and disengagement from life, disillusionment, homelessness, and loss of values and morals. Addiction has also had serious repercussions for the wider community, such as increased levels of crime, violence, sex work, and sexual risk-taking. Many of these are both risk factors and consequences of the drug problem in Liberia.

Seeing the effects that drug addiction has on our youth is heartbreaking. Our young people are in dire straits. Prompt action must be taken to ensure their future and the future of Liberia. As a result of this widespread drug epidemic, our youth have become uncontrollable, self-destructive, abusive, and a threat to the peace and stability of the country.

Worse still, they have been robbed of their opportunities to flourish into the leaders of tomorrow. Our future depends on our youth and there are several things that must be done now in order to secure that future.

First, we need to arise and change the narrative instead of complaining and doing nothing to make change happen.

Next, we must do our best to increase awareness

and understanding of substance abuse and drug-induced psychosis, so we can reduce the stigma associated with drug dependency and the discrimination suffered by substance abusers. This will help parents, families, and communities to provide their drug-addicted young people with the support they require, so they can live Godly lives and fulfil their potential.

We also need to educate our doctors about these things so that they can make better diagnoses and develop proper treatment plans. Steps should be taken to increase the capacity and quality of mental health treatment, including a greater number of mental health professionals and improved infrastructure (psychiatric hospitals).

Most of all, we need to turn back to the Christian principles that guided our country from its inception until, through the upheaval of war, we lost our way. God has a plan and a purpose for our youth. We need to stand on His Word and claim them back for Him.

> For I know the plans I have for you, says the Lord, plans for welfare and not for harm, to give you a future with hope. Then when you call upon me and come and pray to me, I will hear you. When you search for me, you will find me, when you seek me with all your heart.
>
> Jeremiah 29:11–13

Young people of Liberia, the idea that drugs can fix your situation is a lie. They only make things worse. Drug addiction strips you of your integrity and dignity and endangers your life. So, I implore you, if you are struggling with addiction, to reach out to those around you for help and, with God's help, you will overcome. But don't put it off. Though it may be hard, it will be worth it.

Liberians arise and wake up from your slumber. Our children are dying daily. You do not have to be directly affected before you can act. Remember that Liberia is our home – even if we live in foreign parts. If you are Liberian, you will always be Liberian. You will always long for Mama Liberia. So, we cannot let her down. We must rise and address this insidious illness within our country. In God, we have the power to succeed.

Oh Jesus, help us! We need revival and restoration in the land.

> Indeed, the Lord is our helper, and He will help us in our time of need. We stand on the promise of His Word, and, like David, we raise our eyes to the hills. Where will our help come from? Our help comes from the Lord who made heaven and earth.
>
> (Paraphrased from Psalm 121:1–2)

Prostitution

Sadly, since the war, prostitution has become rife in Liberia, with even young girls offering their bodies to men in exchange for food or money. Our culture and traditions around marriage and family have been put to death by war, famine, drugs, and poverty.

Our mothers have been murdered and are no longer around to mentor our daughters in morality. Even those of us who knew better have been forced by circumstance to gag our moral conscience and debase ourselves out of desperation and necessity.

It breaks my heart to see our beautiful women reduced to such a demeaning lifestyle. Girls who ought to be in school have been forced to abandon the classroom to become sex workers simply to survive. How devastating it is to see these young women going through these painful and humiliating experiences. And more so, to realise that they frequently become drug addicts to cope with their lifestyles. They also often turn to crime, stealing extra money from their customers whenever they can, despite the threat of harsh punishments if they are caught.

Often, it is the family that has sent the woman out to "work" as a prostitute because they rely on her income for their survival.

While the government has made some efforts to curtail the act of prostitution, by policing the sector more diligently, this has failed to have much impact. Arresting sex workers – and even publicly shaming them – without addressing the cause, will not solve the problem. As long as our young women do not have the means to get even the most basic standard of living, complete vocational studies or other sponsored programs, and find meaningful employment, they will never be free of the yoke of prostitution.

Crime

Oh Mama Liberia, how many homes have been destroyed by crime? How many innocents are maltreated by criminals? How many of us have lost treasured possessions? Or witnessed the senseless slaying of our family members?

Statistics show that the crime rate in Liberia is currently very high, eighty-one-point-eight percent. It has been steadily growing over the past three years. This is a matter of grave concern to all of us. Why should we live in fear and terror in our own country? Why should Liberians attack and steal from their fellow countrymen and women?

We live behind bars and iron doors. We rush home to be sure we are locked away and safe from criminals by five o'clock in the evening.

Despite the tremendous efforts made by honest police officers, there is too much crime for the police to cope with. They are hopelessly understaffed and underfunded. There appears to be a corrupt element within their ranks that actually assists the criminals or, at least, looks the other way when certain crimes are committed.

When arrests are made, it is difficult to bring the criminals to justice within our overburdened justice system. Here too, corruption rears its ugly head, money changes hands, and all too often, the perpetrators escape justice.

Oh, my sweet Liberia, where is the justice you promised to all men? How long will you continue to treat your own people this way?

Our prisons have become schools of evil and criminality. They should be places where people can regain their humanity and prepare to make positive contributions to their communities.

How could we forget the dark days of the civil war and all the unnecessary bloodshed we endured when so many of us still live with the scars? Do you remember when we were crying unto God for His saving grace? Can you recall the terrible vows we made in exchange for His mercy? How could we forget what God has done for us and become instruments for evil, despising the goodness of God?

> I am the lord thy God, which have brought thee out of Egypt, out of the house of bondage, thou shall have no other gods before Me.
>
> Exodus 20:2–3

Rape

The war is over, and yet we continue to fear for the safety of our girls. The men have become so bad; they think nothing of raping a girl – no matter how young – sparing not a thought to the devastating consequences their actions will have on her life. They have no moral conscience and have become unscrupulous, wicked, and enslaved to their sexuality. Also, they commit these evil deeds and walk away with impunity.

Rape survivors suffer from social isolation, humiliation, low self-esteem, victim-blaming, degradation, and many other psychological and emotional traumas. Besides the many physical and mental traumas suffered by victims of sexual abuse, they are also likely to contract serious and often incurable sexually transmitted diseases.

Illegal emigration

Poverty and a lack of prospects in Liberia are forcing thousands to take their lives into their hands as they attempt to flee the country. They are willing to risk imprisonment and even death for the chance to escape the dire circumstances they live under in their homeland.

Many asylum seekers are duped by Liberian cartels who promise them safe passage into neighbouring countries in exchange for extortionate fees. These shiftless people are nothing more than human traffickers who sell the hapless refugees into slavery across the border. It is not uncommon for these poor people to end up in the sex trade, where they are abused day after day, and anyone who resists or attempts to escape is simply murdered.

Still bleeding

Mama Liberia is still bleeding, even though we do not hear gunfire as often, and people are not running around seeking shelter anymore. Even though there is no civil war, we still see dead bodies in the streets; we still witness suffering and abuse; we still feel fear and frustration. The war is over, and yet we see no justice; we see only more violence; we see only more drugs passing through Liberia; and we see the perpetrators go free. Why are we suffering like this in our own country?

Liberians, it's time for us to ask ourselves the hard question: Is this the purpose God created us for? If we are the oldest independent republic in West Africa, why do we not have anything to show for it except misery and hardship? Why do we continue to mistreat our own people?

Oh, my sweet Liberia, it's time to stand up. Africa is waiting for you. Remember the love of liberty. Remember, you were the light of the continent. It's time to shine. We can do it. But first, we must put away differences, our personal interests, and our pride. We must call for a national revival that will bring us back to our glory days.

Liberia's indomitable spirit

Fourteen years of brutal civil war may have destroyed our country and devastated our people, but the war will not crush our indomitable spirit. We have shown the world that we can endure unimaginable hardship whilst remaining positive and resilient.

Despite our suffering, our dreams and aspirations remain ever hopeful. We will not be overwhelmed by all the terrible things that have happened. Instead, we will look at how far we have come and stay focussed on the light at the end of the tunnel. With clear vision, we will face life's challenges and use our spirit, our creativity, and our innovative skills to build a brighter future for our country.

Once a Liberian, always a Liberian

No matter what, we are proud of Mama Liberia, our native land. She will once again be a place of hospitality and generosity, the perfect place for reflection and growth – the place we called home.

The true beauty of our country lies neither in the ruins we see all around us, nor in the promise of modern infrastructure with gigantic buildings and express road connectivity. It is something far more precious than these things. It is the love we, her people, have for God, for our country, and for one another. Only when we focus on this love and let it shine through us will the rest of the world see Liberia the way we see her.

Love surpasses all, as the Scriptures say:

> You shall love the Lord your God with all your heart and with all your soul and with all your mind. This is the great and first commandment. And a second is like it: You shall love your neighbour as yourself.
>
> Matthew 22:36–40

You can have all the infrastructure and modernisation you like, but if you do not have love, you have nothing. The absence of love leads to disunity, and disunity gives birth to animosity, and animosity develops into atrocities.

A Time for Everything

Now is the time for Liberians to rise from the ashes of war and rebuild a new country, based on the love of God rather than the love of Power.

In Ecclesiastes 3:1–8, the Bible tells us that there is a time for everything.

> There is a time for everything,
> and a season for every activity under the heavens:
> a time to be born and a time to die,
> a time to plant and a time to uproot,
> a time to kill and a time to heal,
> a time to tear down and a time to build,
> a time to weep and a time to laugh,
> a time to mourn and a time to dance,
> a time to scatter stones and a time to gather them,
> a time to embrace and a time to refrain from embracing,
> a time to search and a time to give up,
> a time to keep and a time to throw away,
> a time to tear and a time to mend,
> a time to be silent and a time to speak,

a time to love and a time to hate,
a time for war and a time for peace.

Just as there was darkness before God created the light, so we Liberians have experienced darkness. Now it's time to shine. By putting our hope and our trust in God, we will bring the light and love of Christ into this dark world of ours.

Liberia is a country based on Godly principles. It is time to remember this and align our actions to our beliefs so we can build a robust nation. Instead of focussing on the misdeeds of the past with sorrow and recrimination, it is time for us to turn our eyes towards the future. Let us unite and shoulder the responsibility of restoring Liberia to the beautiful and exceptional country that it once was.

Liberians are truly special people – always smiling, no matter what. Though we are still reeling from the atrocities witnessed during decades of violence, we remain as we have always been – kind, humble, welcoming of foreigners, and totally lacking in aggression. Liberians have always been the sort of people who would get up and dance, even when their stomachs are empty. But with food and jobs scarce, infrastructure, roads, schools, and hospitals non-existent in most of the country, and corruption rife, we have little reason or occasion for smiling or dancing these days. War has changed us, turning a country full of good people against their neighbours.

Liberia used to be one of the finest countries in West Africa, but today it is one of the poorest countries in Africa and the world at large. Despite all our natural resources, many Liberians continue to live in poverty and destitution. Liberians live like strangers in their own country and day-to-day life has become unbearable.

Yet, despite everything that has happened, I love my country, and I feel hopeful about what we as Liberians can achieve. I am sure that one day we will face the future with a smile, although it seems we still have a long way to go.

Arise and shine

Oh, my Liberia, I love you so much! It breaks my heart to see you regressing in this way. My fellow Liberians, let us arise! As it is written in Isaiah 60:1 (NIV),

> Arise, shine, for your light has come and the glory of the Lord rises upon you.

Liberians, it's time to arise! The future of our beloved country depends on you, its citizens. Our forefathers, who gave up their lives for the independence of this country, would be devastated if they saw the terrible state Liberia is in.

Liberians, it's time to arise! We have slept for too long, and the dizziness of sleep has dimmed our eyes. As it is written in Proverbs 6:6–11 (King James Version),

Go to the ant, thou sluggard; consider her ways, and be wise: Which, having no guide, overseer, or ruler, provides her meat in the summer, and gathers her food in the harvest. How long wilt thou sleep, O sluggard? When wilt thou arise out of thy sleep? Yet a little sleep, a little slumber, a little folding of the hands to sleep: So, shall thy poverty come as one that travels, and thy want as an armed man.

As Africa's first and oldest modern republic, Liberia was the first African republic to proclaim its independence, and along with Ethiopia, it was one of only two countries to maintain its sovereignty during colonisation by the West. Yet, we have nothing tangible to show for all the years of independence.

The system has broken down, leaving our people lost in the wilderness; seeking milk and honey; waiting for the change. But when will it come?

Many Liberians have grown tired of waiting and resigned themselves to their lot. As a result, we have become lethargic and complacent.

Liberians, it's time to arise! If we are to achieve anything, we must break out of our trance, get out of our comfort zones and confront our harsh reality.

We have suffered decades of extreme violence. We have been the victims of the war, hunger, thirst, disease, and death that have ravaged our country. We cripple Mama

Liberia while we struggle to reconcile our differences, resolve political issues and ideologies, release outdated affiliations, and put aside the anger, resentment, and hatred of the past.

Have we forgotten the cost of fourteen years of civil war?

Liberians, it's time for us to arise! We are a mighty nation filled with natural beauty, rich resources, fertile soil, and talented individuals. We produced the only African to win soccer's most prestigious award!

Liberians, it's time to arise! The light is ahead. Until we rise, we cannot shine.

APPENDIX

Liberia's diverse population

Liberia's indigenous African population comprises seventeen ethnic groups that make up around ninety-five percent of the total population. These are the Kpelle (the largest group), Kru, Bassa, Grebo, Gio (Dan), Mandingo, Mano, Krahn, Gola, Gbandi, Loma, Kissi, Vai, Sapo, Belleh (Kuwaa), Mende and Dey. Nomadic groups, such as the Fula, and fisherfolk, such as the Fanti, travel between Liberia and her neighbouring countries. Americo-Liberians make up the remaining five percent of the population.

According to the Liberian Constitution, "In order to preserve, foster and maintain the positive Liberian culture, values, and character, only persons who are Negroes or of Negro descent shall qualify by birth or by naturalization to be citizens of Liberia."

However, about five thousand Europeans also settled in Liberia as miners, missionaries and business owners. And a significant number of Lebanese, Indian, and Asian people form part of Liberia's business community. Following the unrest and instability of the civil war, few non-Africans remain in Liberia, with most of them living in and around Monrovia.

The Kpelle

The Kpelle are the largest ethnic group in Liberia. They inhabit Bong County, Bomi County, Gbarpolu County, and Lofa County. This ethnic group also occupies territory in southern Guinea (where they are also known as Guerze) and north-western Cote d'Ivoire. They have a rich agricultural heritage and are hard-working and humble. Each tribe has a chief who is recognised by the government and acts as a mediator on behalf of his tribe.

The Kru

The Kru people form a large ethnic group made up of several sub-ethnic groups in Liberia and Cote d'Ivoire. These include the Bété, Bassa, Krumen, Guéré, Grebo, Klao, Dida, Krahn, and Jabo people.

Kru people live in several counties in the southeast of Liberia, including Grand Kru County, Sinoe County, and River Gee County. Large numbers of Kru fled the war, migrating into Monrovia, where they congregated on Bushrod Island, forming the district known as New Kru Town.

Kru people are mainly Christians, and many of them are Catholic. Their signature dish is palm butter soup served with rice.

Historically, Kru people were prized as traders and sailors on slave ships and were therefore not used as slave labour. But the Europeans found it hard to distinguish them from the other ethnic groups. So, the Kru tattooed their foreheads and the bridges of their noses with blue dye to set themselves apart. They were also notoriously resistant to capture and fought against the abduction of their people into slavery. The Kru along with the Grebo resisted the occupation of Maryland by settlers looking to control their trade.

In modern times, the Kru, Krahn, and Mano people have been the three main indigenous groups involved in Liberia's socio-political activities. Presidents Weah and Sirleaf both had Kru heritage, as did several other notable Liberians.

The Grebo

The Grebo people occupy the south-eastern region of Liberia. They have a very close relationship with the Kru people with whom they share tribal customs. Grebo people are skilled carpenters, making illustrious wood carvings. Grebo artisans make elaborate masks worn on special occasions, such as traditional and cultural assemblies.

In the 1860s and 70s, the Grebo lived in Cote d'Ivoire along the Cavalla River. Some Grebo migrated to Liberia and settled in Cape Palmas, where they encountered American Episcopalian missionaries. The missionaries provided the Grebo with basic education and converted them to Christianity. The Grebo people who remained in Cote d'Ivoire are known as Krumen.

Though Grebo people occupy several counties in

Liberia, they live primarily in Maryland County and Grand Kru County, as well as in River Gee County and Sinoe County. Many Grebo people also live in Petty Town and Doe Community in Monrovia, and in the wider Montserrado County.

Three traditional tribes make up the Grebo people: the Sidibo, the Kimibo, and the Nyekhade. A traditional chief governs each tribe, assisted by an oracle, or high priest, known as a Bodio.

The Grebo were a warring tribe, known for chipping their teeth into ferocious points. In the late 1800s, war broke out between the Grebo and the settlers when the tribe defended their lands and resisted the abduction of their people into the slave trade.

Grebo women are known for their beauty and their luxurious hair growth.

Although some Grebos are Muslim, and some are pagans, most are Christians.

Grebo people love food, especially a dish known as "cha" made from palm butter soup and rice. They also eat peppers with kola nuts – particularly as a "cure-all" for illness.

President William V.S. Tubman was the son of a Grebo-Americo-Liberian. He remained in office for twenty-seven years from 1944 to 1970 – longer than any other Liberian leader.

The Bassa

A subgroup of the larger Kru ethnic, the Bassa mainly occupy the Liberian counties of Grand Bassa, Rivercess, Margibi, and Montserrado. With an overall population of one point five million, they are the second largest ethnic group in the country and the largest in Monrovia.

They have their own language and their own pictographic writing system that has been revived, despite being phased out during the late 1800s. The Bassa people were originally yam, cassava, eddoes, and plantain farmers, as well as being traders and lagoon fishers. They lived in clans, each ruled by its own chief. The clans boasted skilled artisans, including blacksmiths, carvers, weavers, and potters. They are particularly well-known for their intricate brass and wooden masks, and the Brass Finial – an iron rod, plated in brass, featuring a woman's head with five rows of hair that run from front to back, and an encircling herringbone pattern. It is believed to have been the walking stick of Sma Vlen – a mythical ancestor believed to have migrated towards the coast in the sixteenth century.

Following the traditional practices of the neighbouring Dei and Kpelle tribes, the Bassa employed the Port Society and "Gree-Gree" bush methods of educating and initiating children. They also practised Sande, a form of female initiation using helmet masks to represent a primordial female ancestor spirit. This spirit originates from a body of water during a sacred journey by a member official known as a Sowei or sowo. Sande, also known as Bondo, is believed to have originally come from the Mandé people.

The traditional religion of the Bassa people reveres ancestors and supernatural spirits. Since the Bible was first translated into the Bassa language in 1922, they have become predominantly Christian, but have also retained elements of their traditional religion.

The Dei

The Dei ethnic forms part of the Kru language group. They primarily live near the coastal areas of Montserrado County in western Liberia, particularly in the capital Monrovia. The Dei (Dewoin) language is very similar to the Bassa language.

The Gio (Dan)

Mainly based in the city of Man in Cote d'Ivoire, the Dan (also known as the Gio) are members of the southern Mandé ethnic group. The Gio (Dan) migrated from the mountainous regions of West Central Cote d'Ivoire into Nimba County in the early eighteenth century. Known for their art, especially their masks (Ge or Gle), they are the third largest ethnic group in Liberia.

Primarily a farming people, they grow rice, cassava, sweet potatoes, and maize, as well as cash crops such as rubber, cocoa, and coffee. The Gio (Dan) also raise livestock, such as cattle, fowl, sheep, and goats.

In traditional Gio (Dan) culture, men hunt and fish, while women perform domestic duties, such as caring for the children and preparing the meals. Children herd cattle and fend off wild animals and birds from the crops. Their signature dish is "gagba" (called GB), a soup made from cassava, peanut butter, spices, and fresh and dried meats.

Although the Gio (Dan) are predominantly Roman Catholic and Pentecostal Christians, they still observe certain traditional customs and beliefs.

Gio (Dan) men are polygamous, and the culture is patrilineal. Men's societies play a vital role in the socio-political structure of Gio (Dan) communities, particularly as a source of power in the community. All males attend "bon" or bush school, where they undergo initiation into these societies. Women have similar societies into which young women are initiated.

In modern times, many Gio (Dan) communities have become united, while maintaining a fair degree of political independence, under the Leopard Society. Also known as "Gor", this is a society focused on peacemaking between communities which have been in conflict. Individual villages, even those unified under the Leopard Society, still maintain a high degree of political independence.

Gio (Dan) villages are divided into quarters, each headed by a "quarter chief," who could be the oldest male in the family or simply the most aggressive. While the chief administers authority over the entire village, the council of elders holds ultimate sway, assisting the chief in all decisions.

The Mano

The Mano people primarily occupy Nimba County in the north-eastern part of Liberia. They belong to the Zande people. They share many cultural and linguistic similarities with the Gio (Dan). The Mano and the Gio (Dan) form the two largest tribes in Nimba County and often live side-by-side in the same quarter, village, town, or city.

The Manos are multi-talented warriors, as well as being highly skilled musicians, artisans, and artists. In modern day Liberia, they occupy a variety of roles in the government, banking, engineering, and medical sectors. Some of the country's best doctors and engineers are from the Mano ethnic.

Notable Mano people include the late Hon. Jackson F. Doe, who was most likely the true winner of the 1985 presidential and general elections.

The Krahn

The Krahn ethnic are members of the Kru language group. They arrived in an area of Liberia previously known as the "Grain Coast" in the early sixteenth century. Originally hunters, fishers, and farmers, focusing on rice and cassava, the Krahn have, more recently, taken to working in diamond camps and cities, such as Monrovia, or on rubber plantations.

Master Sergeant Samuel Kanyon Doe, Liberia's first indigenous leader and head of state, was a member of the Krahn ethnic group. Through his rise to power, the Krahn became more prominently included in Liberia's government, and many Krahn people migrated into Monrovia. Doe's favouritism towards the Krahn ultimately sparked the first Liberian civil war, in which the Liberian population was strongly divided along ethnic lines, with the Krahn on one side and the Gio (Dan) and Mano on the other.

The Sapo

A subgroup of the Krahn, the Sapo, are also referred to as the Southern Krahn. The Sapo mainly occupy the eastern Liberian regions of Grand Gedeh and Sinoe. Sapo is a Kru language belonging to the Niger-Congo family of languages. Sapo dialects include Juarzon, Kabade (Karbardae), Nomopo (Nimpo), Putu, Sinkon (Senkon), and Waya (Wedjah).

The Gola

The Gola live mostly in western and north-western Liberia. They belong to the Niger-Congo language family. Prominent members of the Gola ethnic group include Charles Taylor, a military warlord who led the NPLC and ruled Liberia from 1997 to 2003. Former president Ellen Johnson Sirleaf's father was Gola and her mother had mixed Kru and German ancestry.

The Gbandi

Also known as the Bandi, Bande, Gbande, or Gbunde, the Gbandi ethnic migrated from the upper Ubangi River in southern Central African Republic and northern Democratic Republic of Congo in the seventeenth century and settled in the northern region of Liberia, now known as Lofa County.

Gbandi people practise Islam and Christianity, as well as retaining some of their traditional beliefs.

Many Gbandi people fled to Guinea during the Liberian Civil War. Notable Gbandi people include the late Dr. Harry Fombah Moniba, who was Vice President Under Samuel K. Doe, and the late Dr. Stephen A. Yekehson, former professor and president of the University of Liberia.

The Loma

The Loma people live mostly in the mountainous parts of Liberia near the Guinean border. They are closely related to the Mende people. Belonging to the Southwestern branch of the Mandé language group, Loma language is similar to Vai, Mende, Kpelle, and Bandi languages.

They are well-known for crafting large wooden masks – the largest being six feet high – decorated with feathers and merging syncretic animal and human designs. In the 1930s, under the guidance of Wido Zobo, and a Loma weaver called Moriba, the Loma developed a written script containing one hundred and eighty-five characters.

Originally agriculturalists, modern-day Loma people enjoy success in the science, medical, and business sectors.

The Kissi

The Kissi belong to the Mel branch of the Niger-Congo language family and primarily occupy Lofa County. Closely related to the Loma and the Kpelle, they are renowned for their basket making and weaving using vertical looms.

They were also famous for their intricate ironwork, most notably the "Kissi penny" – a long iron rod shaped in a "T" at one end, with a hoe-shaped blade at the other. Ranging in length from fifteen to forty centimetres, Kissi pennies circulated widely along the coast of West and Central Africa from around 1880. They continued to serve as valid currency in parts of Liberia until the 1980s.

Although many Kissi are Christians, they also continue to practise their traditional ethnic religion, which includes ancestor worship or praying to deceased relatives. Prior to European contact, the Kissi people produced large numbers of carved soapstone figures and heads. These may have formed part of their ancestor worship and/or represented gods to increase agricultural yields.

As for most Liberian ethnic groups, Kissi children are initiated into poro (male) and sande (female) societies after graduating from bush schools.

Notable Kissi people include former vice president Ambassador Joseph N. Boikai.

The Vai

The Vai are part of the Mandé group of people, and their language is one of the Mandé languages. They live mostly in Pujehun District around the Liberian border, with a small minority living in Sierra Leone. They are known for the development of the Vai syllabary, an early indigenous writing system developed by Chief Momolu Duwalu Bukele and other Vai elders in the 1820s. The Vai people are also very musical, playing many instruments and dancing on special occasions.

Vai education starts with four to five years of bush school, which is divided into the poro (male) and the sande (female) societies. Here, initiates are trained in the Vai traditions, domestic responsibilities and cultural values. They also attend English school to learn the English language.

The Vai people are predominantly Muslim, so their children also attend Quranic schools, where they learn Arabic under the guidance of an Islamic religious leader.

Many Vai practise monotheistic religions, such as Islam and Christianity, alongside their traditional beliefs, which include shamanistic practices to ward off evil spirits and ceremonies for the dead in which food and clothing are left on graves as offerings.

The Vai subsisted on nuts and berries and obtained palm nuts, butter, wine, fuel, soap, and basket weaving materials from palm trees. Traditionally farmers, cultivating rice, cotton, corn, pumpkins, bananas, ginger, coffee, and cocoa; these days, they are more often employed in the clothing, interior design, and furniture industries.

Their signature dish is gbassajama, which is made from ground cassava leaves, braised and tenderised in a broth and mixed with red palm oil stock.

Notable Vai people include Chief Bukele (mentioned above), and former President of Liberia, Ruth Perry (born 1939).

The Kuwaa

The two Kuwaa clans are primarily located in Lofa County in north-western Liberia. They form part of the Kru language group. Kuwaa language is very similar to those of the Lubaisu and Gbade, which are only differentiated by minor variations in pronunciation.

The Mandé

The overarching Mandé ethnic includes groups with a wide variety of cuisines, cultures, and beliefs. Found primarily in the western part of West Africa, they are organised by language and comprise two major groups: East Mandé and West Mandé.

The western branch of the Mandé, known as the Mandinka or Malinke, founded the largest ancient West African empire. Other large Mandé speaking ethnic groups include the Soninke and Susu. Smaller ethnic groups include the Ligbi, Vai, and Bassa.

Today, the Mandé, particularly those who originate

and live in the Sahel regions, are predominantly Muslim and follow a caste system. As traders operating down the river Niger and overland, their influence has spread to neighbouring West African Muslim groups. The Voltaic, Songhai, Fula, Wolof, and Hausa tribes do not speak Mandé. They do, however, maintain varying degrees of similarity with the Mandé-speaking people in terms of their outlook, apparel, culture, and artefacts, including a shared written script, architectural styles, cuisine, and societal norms.

The Americo-Liberians

The Americo-Liberian ethnic group comprises the descendants of African American, Sierra Leone Creole, and Caribbean former slaves, recaptives, and free-born men and women, who settled in Liberia from 1822.

From its independence in 1878 until 1980, Liberia had a one-party system of government. The country was ruled by the True Whig Party (consisting primarily of Americo-Liberians) and the Masonic Order of Liberia.

AUTHOR NOTES

LIBERIAN CULTURE

Hospitality

Liberia has a diverse population, comprising a variety of cultural groups. Some of our ethnic groups have very strong ties to one another and treat each other like family.

Because of our diversity, we are very open and hospitable. Strangers always receive a warm welcome. We have a good relationship with the US, which provides most of the foreign investment we receive.

Despite the horrific inter-ethnic fighting that occurred between the warring factions during the civil wars, most Liberians do not discriminate and are very tolerant of different cultures. We were also known for our exemplary behaviour as refugees in neighbouring countries throughout the war.

Place names

There is no standard spelling for many of the towns in Liberia. This is because these are words in African languages being translated and spelled phonetically.

Sport

Soccer is our national sport. In fact, Liberians love soccer so much that we turn up in huge numbers at every game, and some Liberian men will go without food, just so they can have enough money to buy tickets to see the game.

Liberia has contributed several star players to world soccer, including former president George M. Weah, who won the title of African Footballer of the Year three times in his career. Weah also won the Ballon d'Or, the Onze d'Or, and was named FIFA World Player of the Year in 1995, becoming the first, and currently, the only African player (by FIFA nationality) to win these awards. He is also only the second African-born player to do so. In 1996, Weah came second in the FIFA World Player of the Year rankings and won the FIFA Fair Play Award. In the same year, sports journalists from around the world voted Weah the African Player of the Century.

First female head of state

Liberians also made history in the political arena. Our former president Ellen Johnson Sirleaf was the first elected female head of state in Africa. Sirleaf, a former finance minister under Samuel K. Doe, served as the twenty-fourth Liberian president from 2006 to 2018. Having been awarded the position of Senator of Montserrado County in the 1985 special elections, she was amongst several senators who declined to take up their seats because of controversies surrounding the Samuel K. Doe's self-proclaimed victory.

Liberian women

Liberian women are known for their beauty, charm, and elegance, and especially for their tall stature and naturally pleasing characteristic "Coca-Cola-bottle" body shape. Friendly, outgoing, and easy to get along with, these Liberian beauties usually have high moral standards, which makes it even more heartbreaking that the war stole away our dignity.

Holidays in Liberia

The most celebrated public holiday in Liberia marks the birthday of former president William V.S. Tubman. This holiday is celebrated across the country on 29 November each year. Liberia is surrounded by water, and therefore, we have many beautiful beaches, where we love to while away the holidays. Tubman's birthday is no exception. After a day of fun on the beach, we usually go dancing at one of the many nightclubs in the city.

Liberians love Christmas, and Christmas day is certainly the most joyous holiday of the year. We spend the day with family and friends, exchanging gifts and enjoying delicious home-made food. Often, we will travel to see our loved ones in other parts of the country.

The Christmas season is a time where our focus shifts to our children, and we do everything possible to make Christmas time special for them. We give them lots of gifts and host special Christmas parties just for children. We also arrange special treats for children around Christmas time, such as trips to ice cream shops and children's recreation centres. Some families go on vacation to other countries.

As Liberia has a large Christian population, Christmas is more than just another holiday. It has a deeper spiritual significance to us as the birthday of our King and Saviour, Jesus Christ.

> The next day he [John] saw Jesus coming toward him, and said, "Behold, the Lamb of God, who takes away the sin of the world!"
> John 1:29 (English Standard Version)

Churches across the country lead the celebrations, putting on musical concerts and teaching their congregations about the true meaning of Christmas.

On 26 July each year, Liberians celebrate Independence Day. Usually, the celebrations are spearheaded by our government, and each year, a different county gets the chance to host the Independence Day ceremony. This is a very prestigious occasion attended by government officials, diplomats, international guests, foreign partners, civil rights associations, and many dignitaries – both local and international. The government appoints an orator to give a keynote address on matters of national importance. The spirit of humility and unity amongst all Liberians is a hallmark of this holiday.

Transport

With many accessible and navigable waterways around the country, water travel is a popular form of transport in Liberia. In rural areas, canoes serve both as modes of transport between villages and as fishing craft.

Canoes are constantly whizzing across the waterways with two or three men rowing their passengers to myriad destinations. Taking a canoe from the western side of Monrovia into town or to Bushrod Island is a daily commute for many Liberians. This is a risky form of transport though, as there are seldom any lifejackets available for passengers. If the canoe capsizes, it is likely that pilots, passengers, and possessions will be lost.

We also have more modern forms of transport, including airports and planes, private and commercial cars, motorcycles, and of course, the Keke, which is a three-wheeled semi-enclosed motorised vehicle.

Careers

Many middle- and upper-class Liberians pursue political careers as the vast majority of the population sees politics as an easy pathway to success in Liberia. There are also many entrepreneurs in the country. Many Liberians and foreign residents are employed by private or quasi-government organisations.

Social life

We love nothing more than to unwind and enjoy ourselves, which is why we call Fridays "Super Friday". In our leisure time, and especially on weekends, Liberians converge on the various entertainment centres in and around the city. As a naturally positive and optimistic people, we don't need to rely on others for our happiness. Instead, we do the things we love, and this keeps us happy.

With our generous, outgoing, and caring natures, we love making new friends and helping other people. Those of us who have the means to do so, are extremely generous towards our underprivileged compatriots, helping to take care of children from less fortunate families by sponsoring their education and as well as providing for their welfare – even, occasionally rearing children when their families cannot take care of them themselves.

Despite the immense diversity of languages and cultures across Liberia, we usually get along well. Though our deep compassion, genuine concern for others and trusting nature can make us vulnerable to deception by unscrupulous people.

Long live Liberia! This glorious land of Liberty shall long be ours. Our strength lies in the Lord. If we trust in God, we will prevail.

May Jesus Christ our Lord be with thy spirit. Grace be with us, and the peace of God, which passes all understanding, keep our hearts and minds through Christ Jesus.   –Amen and amen.

Author Bio

Rita Harris lives with her husband Phillip on the Isle of Wight, where she works as a cleaner at the local holiday resort, while Phillip takes care of the house – shopping, cooking, and also doing practical jobs for the neighbours.

Bibliography

The author would like to acknowledge the following sources:

Demographics of Liberia

https://www.cs.mcgill.ca/~rwest/wikispeedia/wpcd/wp/d/Demographics_of_Liberia.htm#:~:text=There%20are%2016%20ethnic%20groups,of%20immigrants%20from%20the%20U.S

Distances between places in Liberia

https://www.google.com/maps/dir/Gardnersville,+Dabwe+Town,+Liberia/Cuttington+University,+2CRW%2B5FC,+Phebe,+Liberia/@6.6880288,-10.8048126,9z/data=!3m1!4b1!4m14!4m13!1m5!1m1!1s0xf09f8e24247f129:0x54214215c54faed!2m2!1d-10.739822!2d6.336855!1m5!1m1!1s0xfa65e2d06df45cd:0xcae4e49f52ad07eb!2m2!1d-9.5538568!2d7.0404482!3e0?entry=ttu

Ancient history of Liberia

https://en.wikipedia.org/wiki/Liberia

https://en.wikipedia.org/wiki/Oldowan

History of Liberia

https://en.wikipedia.org/wiki/History_of_Liberia

https://en.wikipedia.org/wiki/Liberian_Declaration_of_Independence

https://www.gutenberg.org/ebooks/11353
https://www.gutenberg.org/ebooks/54542
https://drive.usercontent.google.com/download?id=1Nyej5Durdbckdy-qagYOWDjE5H6DqSo3&export=download&authuser=0&confirm=t&uuid=5d2f72ec-32f8-475e-86b0-12e8f7d618eb&at=APZUnTUesuft83hVkaIqUfkvoAA:1691812908337

Timeline of events

Author's note: The exact order of events differed in some of the sources I consulted. I have drawn on my personal recollection of events and the data from what appeared to be the most reliable sources to recreate the timeline in this book.

https://www.bbc.com/news/world-africa-13732188
https://reliefweb.int/report/liberia/liberia-chronology-25-years-conflict-and-turmoil?gclid=Cj0KCQjw_5unBhCMA RIsACZyzS3zdbJBVGGNXd0gDkWAN13TwndAAprvmv U8632U_uiyRK9l-8QxvQ8aAp0sEALw_wcB
https://www.encyclopedia.com/education/news-wires-white-papers-and-books/sawyer-amos-1945
https://web.archive.org/web/20070308142809/http://www.c-r.org/our-work/accord/liberia/chronology.php#1990

Tolbert's presidency

https://liberiainfo.co/prd/the-last-whig/
https://ecfr.eu/special/african-cooperation/mano-river-union/#:~:text=The%20objective%20is%20also%20to,promote%20social%20and%20cultural%20affairs
https://theorganiser.net/africa/4438-liberia-april-12-2022-marked-the-42nd-anniversary-of-the-death-of-president-wr-tolbert

https://www.nytimes.com/1973/02/04/archives/liberia-expands-agricultural-output.html

The Rice Riots

http://www.globalsecurity.org/military/library/report/1985/liberia_1_riceriots.htm

https://allafrica.com/stories/200808150432.html

https://en.wikipedia.org/wiki/Progressive_Alliance_of_Liberia#cite_note-2

Political power in Liberia pre- and post-war

https://web.archive.org/web/20110823005017/http://nationalreforms.com/democracy-watch/liberia-two-party-electoral-system-is-the-best-option.html

Coup by Samuel Doe

https://en.wikipedia.org/wiki/1980_Liberian_coup_d%27%C3%A9tat

https://en.wikipedia.org/wiki/People%27s_Redemption_Council

https://www.washingtonpost.com/archive/politics/1980/04/26/liberia-detains-businessmen-sets-martial-law/6e6e75cf-c23d-470a-ad0e-71cf94c3834b/

Samuel K. Doe's presidency

https://en.wikipedia.org/wiki/Samuel_Doe

https://www.ictj.org/sites/default/files/ICTJ-Liberia-Brief-History-2006-English.pdf

https://www.washingtonpost.com/archive/politics/1986/07/24/liberian-president-doe-woos-worlds-lenders/49bbcf43-77fd-4dfb-9519-4b622113a5db/

Quiwonkpa's attempted coup

https://en.wikipedia.org/wiki/Thomas_Quiwonkpa

Charles Taylor

https://www.newyorker.com/news/news-desk/charles-taylor-and-the-killing-tree

https://www.propublica.org/article/firestone-and-the-warlord-chapter-3]

Charles Taylor's attack on Butuo

https://www.refworld.org/docid/45cc8f5c2.html

https://academic.oup.com/book/44040/chapter-abstract/373132975?redirectedFrom=fulltext

Charles Taylor's later years

https://reliefweb.int/report/liberia/liberating-liberia-charles-taylor-and-rebels-who-unseated-him

https://www.nytimes.com/1992/04/14/world/in-liberia-s-illusory-peace-rebel-leader-rules-empire-of-his-own-design.html

Assassination of Samuel K. Doe

https://www.theafricareport.com/144562/pt-5-liberia-samuel-doe-death-washed-down-with-budweiser/

https://en.wikipedia.org/wiki/Samuel_Doe#:~:text=The%20First%20Liberian%20Civil%20War,Johnson%20on%209%20September%201990
Burial: https://allafrica.com/stories/200808290064.html

Amos Sawyer
https://www.encyclopedia.com/education/news-wires-white-papers-and-books/sawyer-amos-1945

The Civil War
https://www.hrw.org/reports/1993/liberia/
https://en.wikipedia.org/wiki/First_Liberian_Civil_War
https://en.wikipedia.org/wiki/Monrovia_Church_massacre
https://en.wikipedia.org/wiki/Charles_Taylor_(Liberian_politician)
Africa Watch, Liberia: A Human Rights Disaster, News from Africa Watch (New York: Africa Watch, 26 October 1990), p. 1.

Cease fires and peacekeeping forces.
https://peacekeeping.un.org/sites/default/files/past/unomilFT.htm
https://www.c-r.org/accord/liberia/bringing-peace-liberia
https://jmss.org/article/download/57806/43480
https://asq.africa.ufl.edu/wp-content/uploads/sites/168/ASQ-Vol-4-Issue-1-Tuck.pdf

NPRAG

https://www.nytimes.com/1992/04/14/world/in-liberia-s-illusory-peace-rebel-leader-rules-empire-of-his-own-design.html

https://www.google.com.au/books/edition/West_Africa_s_Security_

Civil unrest in 1991

https://www.hrw.org/reports/1991/liberia/#8
https://www.hrw.org/reports/1991/liberia/#16

US involvement

https://acrobat.adobe.com/link/review?uri=urn:aaid:scds:US:cc8c5cc9-0051-307e-80d1-ff33bb66d471

https://acrobat.adobe.com/link/review?uri=urn:aaid:scds:US:aec85d39-25e7-36a0-a61c-dab497d4de9d

https://www.marines.mil/Portals/1/Publications/On%20Mamba%20Station%20--%20U.S.%20Marines%20in%20West%20Africa,%201990-2003%20PCN%2019000413300_PART_1.pdf

https://permanent.fdlp.gov/gpo145835/B_0164_HAHN_TWO_CENTURIES_OF_US_MILITARY_OPERATIONS_IN_LIBERIA_CHALLENGES_OF_RESISTANCE_AND_COMPLIANCE.PDF

The Black Berets

https://frontpageafricaonline.com/editorial/berets-are-resurfacing-in-liberia-warranting-a-serious-cause-for-concern/?fbclid=IwAR3NUi2n40pQq3nsSYxZI3CqMQFV4NJr

3tl-Hrb778lD7M9yp0_PfEL6EeU
https://www.theperspective.org/articles/0202200601.html
https://www.hrw.org/reports/1993/liberia/#5

Child soldiers
https://www.theatlantic.com/magazine/archive/1992/12/liberia/376354/
https://link.springer.com/article/10.1007/s10597-017-0154-3#ref-CR18 - Human Rights Watch (HRW). (2004). How to Fight, How to Kill: Child Soldiers in Liberia. Human Rights Report A1602: https://www.hrw.org/report/2004/02/02/how-fight-how-kill/child-soldiers-liberia
https://www.slate.com/articles/news_and_politics/dispatches/features/2007/liberia_recovers_from_war/a_boy_soldier_grows_up.html

Operation Octopus
https://www.theperspective.org/octopus.html
https://www.refworld.org/docid/3ae6a6088.html
https://www.propublica.org/article/firestone-and-the-warlord-chapter-6
https://www.theadvocatesforhumanrights.org/res/byid/9358

Real-life accounts of human rights atrocities by both sides
https://www.usip.org/publications/2006/02/truth-commission-liberia

https://www.jstor.org/stable/41852974

https://www.theadvocatesforhumanrights.org/res/byid/9358

https://www.pbs.org/frontlineworld/stories/liberia/facts.html

https://www.newyorker.com/news/news-desk/charles-taylor-and-the-killing-tree

Sierra Leone

https://www.unhcr.org/news/briefing-notes/liberia-sierra-leonean-returns

The legacy of war

https://www.pbs.org/frontlineworld/stories/liberia/facts.html

Post-war Liberia

https://www.dignityliberia.org/liberia-a-nation-in-recovery.html

Substance abuse in post-war Liberia

https://link.springer.com/article/10.1007/s10597-017-0154-3

https://www.tandfonline.com/doi/abs/10.1080/17542863.2011.583737

https://www.unodc.org/documents/justice-and-prison-reform/ReducingReoffending/Liberian_United_Youth_for_Community_Safety_and_Development_LUYCD.pdf

Human Capital Gap

https://www.worldbank.org/en/news/press-release/2022/09/27/liberia-economic-update-prospects-for-inclusive-and-sustainable-growth#:~:text=By%20 2020%2C%20the%20human%20capital,outcomes%20 are%20multiple%20and%20complex

Crime rate in Liberia

https://www.numbeo.com/crime/country_result.jsp?country=Liberia

Hunger statistics

https://www.globalhungerindex.org/liberia.html

Diverse Culture of Liberia

https://en.wikipedia.org/wiki/Liberia#Demographics
https://web.archive.org/web/20080625062344/http://www.cal.org/co/liberians/liberian_050406_1.pdf
https://www.refworld.org/docid/4954ce5823.html#:~:text=Liberia's%20first%20inhabitants%20 were%20ancestors,from%20the%20north%20and%20east.
https://en.wikipedia.org/wiki/Kpelle_people
https://en.wikipedia.org/wiki/Bassa_(Liberia)
https://en.wikipedia.org/wiki/Mano_people
https://en.wikipedia.org/wiki/Gio_people
https://en.wikipedia.org/wiki/Kru_people
https://en.wikipedia.org/wiki/Grebo_people
https://en.wikipedia.org/wiki/Krahn

https://en.wikipedia.org/wiki/Vai_people
https://en.wikipedia.org/wiki/Gola_people
https://en.wikipedia.org/wiki/Mandinka_people
https://en.wikipedia.org/wiki/Mende_people
https://en.wikipedia.org/wiki/Kissi_people
https://en.wikipedia.org/wiki/Gbandi
https://en.wikipedia.org/wiki/Loma_people
https://en.wikipedia.org/wiki/Mane_people
https://en.wikipedia.org/wiki/Americo-Liberian_people

www.ingramcontent.com/pod-product-compliance
Lightning Source LLC
Chambersburg PA
CBHW051423290426
44109CB00016B/1414